GIVE HER SIX

GIVE HER SIX

A Distillery Manager's Son in 1960s Bruichladdich

GRAHAM LOGIE

BROWN DOG BOOKS

First published 2023

Published under licence by Brown Dog Books and
The Self-Publishing Partnership Ltd, 10b Greenway Farm, Bath Rd, Wick,
nr. Bath BS30 5RL

www.selfpublishingpartnership.co.uk

ISBN printed book: 978-1-83952-684-8
ISBN e-book: 978-1-83952-685-5

Cover design by Kevin Rylands
Internal design by Andrew Easton

Printed and bound in the UK

This book is printed on FSC® certified paper

MIX
Paper | Supporting responsible forestry
FSC® C013604

This book is for :

My sisters **Patricia McMillan** and **Norma Sinclair**

Thank you for your help, photographs and advice, but mainly for being my sisters.

My partner **Lesley Dawn Fotheringham**

When we met, your dancing and show business career fascinated me. The list of entertainers you've worked with reads like a Who's Who of television icons we watched in the 70s and 80s. The concept of this book started when you said you couldn't imagine what life was like growing up on a small island. Keep getting stronger.
Thank you for your support.

My daughter **Julie Hemsley**

Always there for me, hope this makes you proud.

Bruichladdich's **Mary McGregor**

Your book inspired this book. Thank you.

Contents

INTRODUCTION

Having been inspired by other books about tales of Islay life, I thought I'd offer my memories of my childhood in Bruichladdich from 1961 onwards, not only from a child's perspective, but as the local Distillery Manager's son.

From four to fifteen years of age, it's not just a view of island life, but very much centred in the village itself.

Every decade will have it's own unique differences and ways of life and I just feel fortunate to have grown up witnessing very different periods before and after the introduction of roll-on/roll-off ferries.

Life in the early sixties seemed so straightforward and uncomplicated, with a much slower pace and great freedom for children around the village, and indeed in workplaces like the distillery, the pier, coal yard, and crofts.

I also had quite a unique opportunity to return to Islay to work at the same job as my father, but at a different distillery many years later, only to leave the island for a second time, after experiencing how much distilleries and distilling companies had changed.

In today's age of electronic games and mobile telephones that occupy youngsters, I'm sure readers will be surprised at what simple lives we had as 60s children and how we never became bored with simple pleasures like sitting in a lorry all day or helping on crofts or boats. One thing that became apparent to me when making recollections, was that we never disobeyed anything we were asked to do by any adult in the village. We certainly weren't cheeky to any of the men in the village because if they didn't give you a clip round the ear, they'd make damn sure my parents got to know about it. Again, being the Manager's son, Dad always had high expectations of me and hated the thought of me showing him up.

I enjoyed some of the research involved, especially around boats that were our lifeline for many years. No-one could help falling in love with puffers, each one having it's own characteristics. My own favourite was the 'Raylight.' As you'll read later, the title **Give her Six** stems from the shout from puffer deckhands when they wanted the winch operated at full speed. As children, we didn't really have any idea where puffers came from, who loaded them, where did the cargoes originate from. We just knew that as soon as a speck appeared on the horizon at the mouth of Lochindaal, they were coming to Bruichladdich, and chapters in the book will tell of our involvement with them.

We've all heard Dan McPhail's song, sung on the 'Vital Spark' about 'The Crinan Canal for me.' Again, as children, none of us appreciated that such a feat of engineering as the Crinan Canal existed to ease the passage for such boats, sailing from the Clyde to the islands, bypassing the heavier seas off the Mull of Kintyre.

While researching some dates proved extremely interesting, I was also saddened to read of the fate of a lot of boats that had become household names to us.

My biggest regret is probably finding out that, after her service to Islay, Jura and Gigha, the mail boat 'Lochiel' had been converted into a floating restaurant in Bristol. I had so many opportunities to visit her during part of my RAF career in South Wales, practically an hour's drive away, but I didn't think to enquire what became of the boats and had just never appreciated that there was a life for them after serving us.

Even more surprising was reading of some boats who either perished, or went on to give long service in some very unexpected parts of the world such as Honduras, Spain and the Greek islands. We just seemed to think of them as 'our' boats.

In writing about village life, I also wanted to show what small differences and opportunities arose being the Distillery Manager's son. In those days, distilleries were the sort of focal part of villages and the Managers were in a pretty responsible position within the community. The vast majority of employees of distilleries lived within the boundaries of the villages so really, work and leisure time were very much connected.

I did get more access to the distillery than other children and my memories proved invaluable in later life when I became a Distillery Manager myself. Visitors on Islay, and whisky enthusiasts I gave presentations to around the world, were always fascinated to hear of traditions and family history, so talking of my childhood in Bruichladdich gave me a lot of credibility and folk wanted to hear of such connections in what was (and sadly isn't now) a very traditional industry.

I remember giving my first whisky presentation in Japan in 2003. Totally untrained, just thrown in at the deep end, and accompanied by an interpreter, I rattled off a ninety minute talk on the brands, tasting notes of the whiskies and the production methods unique to each distillery.

Afterwards, I asked our company's local Tokyo marketing manager if he thought the presentation was what he wanted from me, and he said it was OK.

I thought it was better than OK, but he explained that if I wanted to do a ninety minute presentation in Japan, and I wanted the full attention of every attendee to totally buy into it, then the first twenty minutes has got to be about me. Only then would I be accepted and listened to intently. So having such strong distillery connections throughout my childhood in Bruichladdich fascinated the Japanese who then just wanted to absorb every sentence.

While not wanting to slate the multi national companies that own huge parts of the Scotch Whisky industry nowadays, I know they offer huge opportunities around the world, and reading my company's career website, I could have plied my trade in Australian rum distilleries, African Guinness breweries, or Californian vineyards. Similarly, when a visitor steps off a bus in Scotland, they can be greeted by a manager or guide of any nationality. Great fun for those who seek to venture, but having been immersed in traditional whisky culture since the day I was born, I find it terribly hard not to be very disappointed that this romantic industry has moved on.

In one chapter, I refer to a whisky podcast I made during Feis 2010. In it, I mentioned that my father only ever saw one career path for me, and that was as a Distillery Manager. Of course, as a young man, I thought I knew better so after a couple of years as a distillery warehouseman, he mentioned about me starting to move up the career ladder, so his hot headed son left home and joined the RAF. Of course, after I finished my twelve years service, I couldn't wait to get back into distilling in my own time and at my own choice, and eventually I got the Manager's role that he sought for me.

It was a very proud time for both of us when he visited me at Talisker Distillery on the Isle of Skye in 2002, and it was my turn, as Manager, to show him round, before his sad passing in 2003.

One thing I never imagined, and never anticipated was the extent of copyright law. Writing this book took practically three weeks, although nobody saw much of me in that time, but tracing photographs and their owners easily took up another three months of my time. I just have to say how indebted I am to people, museums, historical societies etc that rallied round me to help without any thought of financial gain. Interestingly, I was astounded at how many contributors, after they'd cleared it with me to use their pictures, then recalled stories of their own experiences of holidaying and whisky tasting on Islay.

Although the title of my book refers to my childhood, I took the opportunity to finish with some tales of me returning to Islay when the opportunity arose for me to be transferred through my work.

Distilling life in the sixties and the noughties is like chalk and cheese but I am glad I experienced both.

Chapter One - The Move

Prior to our move to Islay, we lived at Royal Brackla Distillery, south of Nairn. My Dad Peter, Mum May, big sister Patricia (Tish) and I lived in a distillery cottage at the road-end leading into the distillery, beside the very picturesque distillery dam.

Apart from a short spell in National Service with the Royal Navy, mostly in the Pacific Ocean, Dad worked in distilleries all his life, starting as a stoker at coal-fired Benromach Distillery in his native town of Forres. Perhaps due to his spell in the Navy, and seeing so much of the world, he was always ambitious and wanted to better himself. Distilleries of the day had much larger employee numbers than nowadays, and there was much more loyalty to companies and distilleries, so vacancies were few and far between and the way to get better paid jobs and promotions was not to be afraid to relocate.

His first move was to Glenlochy Distillery in Fort William, followed by a further relocation to Ardmore Distillery in Kennethmont, south of Huntly, before returning to Morayshire for a production shift job as stillman at Brackla.

Consequently, and probably unusually for the majority of families, myself and my two sisters were all born in different parts of Scotland (Forres, Aberdeen and Glasgow) when Mum and Dad were based at Fort William, Kennethmont and, eventually, Bruichladdich respectively.

Mum, originally from Elgin, became quite quickly used to the lifestyle of moving every few years and the neatly stacked pile of wooden tea chest boxes in our various sheds over the years was testament to her organisation for every move. She always talked fondly of everywhere they'd lived, even rainy Fort William at the foot of Ben Nevis, where they shared their first marital home. It's always easy to think that your parents know everything, but you forget that they went through all the same learning and life experiences as we do. Funniest story Mum would admit to, and you had to listen to this every time we had rice pudding for tea, was as a new bride, she boiled pudding rice as a surprise for Dad coming home from work. She gently boiled the rice in water, but impatiently waited for the rice to expand. Always fearing that it wasn't going to expand enough to make two decent size platefuls, she added more and more rice, but when it soaked the water up and properly expanded, it gushed over the top of the pan and all over the cooker. 'I just thought it was never going to stop,' she always said.

As I said, always ambitious, Dad decided to apply for, and got, his first Distillery Manager position at Bruichladdich Distillery, owned by A.B. Grant & Co. It's hard to imagine the logistics of living in Nairnshire in 1960 and applying for a job where the head office was in Glasgow, and the Manager's job was on Islay, the most southerly of the Inner Hebrides off Scotland's west coast. There were no computers, no internet, no mobile phones, I imagine no house phone, and he couldn't drive, so quite a challenge to tie everything together. In today's world, an online vacancies advertisement and application form, a Zoom call for an interview, book your CalMac ferry tickets online and before you know it, you've moved from one end of Scotland to another. That's a bit simplistic but it shows how technology has made life so much easier, but less personal. Writing down my memories, I find that it is only now that I stop to appreciate what was involved. As a child, eating and playing were my priorities, and none of the above entered my mind.

As I was just over five years of age, I only have a few vivid memories of life at Royal Brackla Distillery, prior to us moving to Bruichladdich.

One memory would probably horrify healthy food enthusiasts nowadays, but lunch on a Saturday was always sausage and mashed tatties (potato). Mum always served up the meal and quick as a flash, I arranged my tatties into a rounded form with a hole in the centre. I had anticipated Mum asking, 'Who wants sausage bree?' I thought it was heaven having the liquid from the frying pan poured into my tatties and then taking great care to mix the two together. Of course, I now know that sausage bree was melted lard and while it is unlikely to be recommended in today's health-conscious environment, it was blooming delicious.

Two other tales from Brackla. I think you'll quickly get the gist that food plays a big part in my life.

In the North of Scotland, a sandwich is known as a 'piece' and apparently that was the first word I ever spoke before mundane things like 'Mummy' or 'Daddy'. I've been told that when Dad came into the house at about 6.10 am after his nightshift, I'd be standing in my cot, both hands gripped on the upright bars, like a prisoner at a cell window, shouting, 'Piece, piece.' In my eyes, I was just making sure everyone knew I was awake and it was breakfast time.

My family take great delight in also telling the story of my first day at Cawdor Primary School. Tish took me to see the school last year and assured me we walked the one-mile stretch of road from Brackla every day. I have no recollection at all, but it's a very winding narrow road, very similar to roads around Bruichladdich. The morning class done, the school lunch eaten, then it was playtime. That's when myself and the Distillery Customs Officer's son, Andrew Hines, decided to go out of the playground and down to the local burn to play. Obviously there were no CCTV cameras, intercoms or locked gates like today's schools.

We became totally absorbed in exploring and quite forgot about time. We returned late and as soon as we entered the corridor and heard the teacher's voice, we realised our class had already begun, and we were wise enough to know that we were meant to be in the classroom. So we crept up to the door outside the classroom and peeked through its glass panels and a wee girl shouted to the teacher, 'There they are, Miss.' We didn't exactly need someone highlighting our stupidity. I don't remember the teacher's reaction, but Mum couldn't have made an issue of it because if I was scolded at home I'd have remembered it, and now come to think of it, classes had restarted without any search party looking for two missing four-year-olds.

So Mum, Dad, Tish and I moved to Bruichladdich in January 1961. The journey is a total blur to me, but Tish told me that we all flew to Islay. That alone would have been quite an adventure to a child in the early 60s, especially as the most exciting thing I'd ever done prior to that was travel from Brackla to Nairn on a Bluebird service bus with Mum. Actually, my very first visual memory of Bruichladdich is standing beside the whitewashed wall beside the Distillery boiler house with Dad and I remember a woman saying to me, 'Are you enjoying the school?' and Dad straight away came out with a saying that he often repeated, 'Well it's up to himself, better to become a doctor than a docker.'

Moving home so often has plusses and minuses, especially moving away from friends you made, but having the opportunity to move to Islay turned out to be the best thing that ever happened to us all. We've introduced so many other family members, who would never have had the opportunity or inclination to visit the island.

Mr A.B. Grant (right).

Credit – Family photo.

Part of the deal to encourage Dad to take on the job at Bruichladdich Distillery was that a new house was to be built for us, but the construction had barely started when we arrived, only the foundation had been laid. Above the filling store at the distillery was an apartment, known as the Flat, normally exclusively used by visiting directors and dignitaries, and this was to become our home for several months until our new house was built. I remember two names of Company VIPs who periodically visited - Mr A.B. Grant, the owner and Miss Thomson, one of the directors. I remember Mum telling me that Mr Grant was a millionaire, but I probably had no idea what that meant other than he was very rich. I don't suppose I'd even seen my first ten shilling (50p) note, let alone try and envisage what a million pounds was. I remember seeing more of Miss Thomson (none of us, Dad included, ever referred to the VIPs by their first names), and she always looked so glamorous in stylish dresses and Sophia Loren type sunglasses. We could always tell when the dignitaries were visiting because Dad wore a suit to work. That's a great thing about island life, your bosses can't sneak up on you unannounced, they have to book the ferry or plane.

BRUICHLADDICH casks on what was our front lawn.

Credit – Dave Shea (via Flickr).

Our house was finally finished in the summer of 1961. It was a Dorran bungalow which was basically a sectional prefabricated building, popular in the 50s, 60s and early 70s, and quick and easy to construct. R.G. Tarran was a Hull-based company that took over a dyeworks building from the infamous Pullars of Perth to produce the Dorran bungalow range which proved very popular in Argyllshire and many could be seen when driving from Tarbert to Inveraray. Although it was a lovely house, as a child I wasn't really interested in construction techniques, but the Dorrans had poor insulation, and the steel pins and bolts holding the sections together corroded over the years due to the condensation. Hence our house isn't standing any more. The land which was our house and garden, for Bruichladdich Distillery enthusiasts, is where the casks bearing the name B-R-U-I-C-H-L-A-D-D-I-C-H are now situated. On the north side of our house was our neighbour Neil McLachlan's croft. On the south side were the main distillery buildings. Across the quiet road in front of the house was the seashore, and behind was an open field, so just the ideal play area for a wee boy. We had a fabulous view across Lochindaal to Bowmore and also looked directly onto the pier at Bruichladdich. As you'll see from some anecdotes later in the book, having a good view of the pier was lovely if you were interested in seeing boats, but a real hindrance if you were a wee boy playing on the pier and not wanting your mother to be able to see how dangerous some of your antics were. Obviously now I fully appreciate the danger of children trying to step onto a boat which was swaying on the waves, and I'd be horrified to think of my grandchildren attempting that, but we knew no fear, only adventure. The boats' crews and the men working on the pier were always too busy to watch us, and in fact sometimes encouraged us

Dorran bungalow nearing completion.

Credit – Family photo.

to jump on board the boats to perhaps check on how much cargo was left deep in the hold.

In the following chapters, I tell of the advantages of being the Manager's son, but to a boy, there were disadvantages too. In particular, if a company VIP was visiting, and travelling alone, Dad would feel obliged to entertain them at our house in an evening. This was really an extension to the business talks they'd held during the day, and general gossip about the distilling industry, and I suppose the guest was interested to see the house that the company had invested in. Mum and Tish appeared to be cleverer than me, and never seemed to be around on those evenings, but I was encouraged (forced) to sit all evening in the front room while the men had a dram and talked nothing but business. Worse still, the TV was always respectfully switched off and every now and again I'd be asked what I wanted to do when I grew up or what subjects interested me at school. I was about nine or ten years old, so in my mind, my interests right at that second were, when are you leaving?, what are we having for supper?, and why has the TV got to be off?

After several months, Mum was finding it harder to adjust to island life than the rest of us. She was born and raised in Elgin and although a couple of their distillery cottages had been in the countryside, she just found it difficult to settle. So Dad said to give it a year and if she was still uneasy, he'd return to the mainland to find work. Dad's new job entitled him to a company car so he quickly passed his driving test and our first car was a green Morris Minor, then a red Triumph Herald, followed by a brown Humber Sceptre (Registration No BSN 355 C, funny how some small details stick in your mind) which meant on Saturdays we could go to the bigger shops in Bowmore and Port Ellen. Shops we used regularly were for example Islay Farmers on the outskirts of Bowmore, Bobby Hodkinsons at the top of the pier, McIlwraith's clothes shop and

Sutherlands on Shore Street for general goods.

Sutherland's fascinated me because upstairs there was a large selection of vinyl records for sale and I used to watch the young working men from around the island choosing the current hits every week. I used to dream that one day I could have long hair like them and be really cool buying my choice of records.

Across School Street from Bowmore Distillery there was a large wooden building housing a snooker hall and a barber's shop. It was really dark and dingy inside, but fortnightly, totally against my will, Dad dragged me inside for us both to get our hair cut. After getting my hair cut first, and then the obligatory smothering in Brylcreem, I had to sit and wait, and this was the only place I genuinely heard this, but after his trim I used to hear Dad being asked, 'Something for the weekend, Mr Logie?' My young mind innocently thought, 'How does he know what we're doing this weekend?'

Quickly Mum came to love Islay, joining the WRI and meeting lots of others, and having a couple of her friends in the village round to the house for a cuppa in the afternoons, and the only reason they left the island in 1972 was because Dad got a promotion. Invergordon Distillers had taken over Bruichladdich Distillery in 1968 and they moved him to jointly manage Tullibardine Distillery and Deanston Distillery in Perthshire. Mum and Dad returned to retire and live in Bowmore in 1999 so there is a definite lure back to the island.

Television was still very much a novelty and because we were at the edge (fringe) of the normal TV signal range from masts located on the mainland, Fringe Model TVs were required and as well as receiving inferior quality pictures for much of the time, there were two disadvantages of weak signals. If something emitting a signal came directly between you and the TV mast, it became the stronger signal,

Many a summer's evening we'd be watching the news at home, and next minute there would be a crackly conversation between two fishing boat skippers. We were powerless to do anything about it until they moved on.

Another interruption to the TV signal, more local than fishing boats, was interference caused by vehicles. I remember, every Friday at about 5.30 pm, a vehicle would pass the house and Dad, with his back to the window, said, 'That'll be MacBrayne's bloomin' lorry back from Port Ellen.' Friday was Port Ellen's turn to have the cargo boat call in, so the squad from Bruichladdich pier went to Port Ellen in their lorry to lend a hand for the day. Only some vehicles on the island caused the interference, but we could identify each vehicle before we'd even seen it, by the sound and severity of the crackling noise on the television.

A hindrance caused by the weaker signals was that we struggled to tune into ITV. The BBC signal from the mainland was stronger. We could actually get a better ITV signal from Northern Ireland (Ulster TV), but watched it less because we didn't get Scottish news or current affairs and many programmes were focused on the troubles in Northern Ireland. Plus, of course, Dad had a crush on Mary Marquis who used to present the news on BBC Scotland at 6 pm so no way was any other channel going to even be considered. Many times over the last five decades, people have mentioned a programme from the 60s and expected me to have seen it as a child, but if it was on ITV, I probably didn't.

I now live near Bath in Somerset and often I pass the town of Keynsham, near Bristol. Every time I see the road signs, I'm reminded of the many evenings we spent in Bruichladdich when, if the TV reception was too bad, we just turned it off. As Dad was always busy doing something, Mum, Tish and I would tune into Radio Luxembourg, one of the first commercial radio stations, emitting super-strong signals from the Grand Duchy of Luxembourg, across Europe, much to the annoyance of the UK Government who had given the BBC a monopoly of radio broadcasting from UK territory, and had prohibited all forms of radio advertising. As well as playing the Top Twenty records that we all loved, one advertisement always sticks in my mind and that was Horace Batchelor, a well-spoken and extremely convincing gentleman who invited listeners to follow his method of winning on the Football Pools. To take advantage of his 'Famous Infra-Draw Method' you had to send your football pools coupon predictions to him, by post, and he would decide the best way to enter your coupon. Horace became more infamous than some of the top DJs of the day, including Alan Freeman and Pete Murray, and a measure of his success was that he retired to a 27-bedroom house, and estimated his winnings at £12 million in 1977. Horace lived in Keynsham (pronounced Cane Sham), and several times during a broadcast he'd read out his address on the radio: Horace Batchelor, Department 1, Keynsham, spelt K-E-Y-N-S-H-A-M, Bristol. Often he repeated this two or three times (K-E-Y-N-S-H-A-M, that's K-E-Y-N-S-H-A-M), virtually his catchphrase, so it stuck in my mind. If you nowadays search for Horace on the Internet, his catchphrase of spelling the word Keynsham is actually mentioned before anything about his life and work. After Horace sadly passed away, there was a local Police Sergeant who was interviewed on the radio and was asked if he had any comical tales from the Police Station. He told how one evening, a Police Constable was despatched to an incident at a house in Keynsham. When the Constable returned to the station, the Sergeant asked him what it had been about. The Constable replied, 'Oh, that house I was sent to was Horace Batchelor's. He's dead, D-E-A-D, dead.

Myself, Dad and Tish with Triumph Herald.

No 7 warehouse (which collapsed into garden) in background.

Credit – Family photo.

Modern building regulations would probably not permit such a thing now, but in the early 60s we had a bonded warehouse (No. 7) built about thirty yards behind our house, at the end of the garden. The building of the warehouse didn't particularly interest me, although I do remember thinking it odd that the brickwork on the gable end, closest to our house was completed right to the top and looked fragile and unsupported, while the rest of the walls were in progress but slightly further behind. It just looked odd compared to other buildings I'd seen before, where all the walls of a building rose from the ground together. I slept in a back bedroom of the house, facing the warehouse, and one early morning (Dad was at work, Mum and Tish were in the kitchen), the entire gable wall collapsed into our garden. I was still asleep, but Tish tells me they had the kitchen curtains closed, and there was a dull thud outside. Unfortunately, the night watchman was quite seriously hurt as he was in his little shed at the foot of the gable end. Several workmen were seen running towards the little shed so they knew straight away that something was wrong. I never heard a thing, surprisingly, and only knew about it when Mum woke me for school. I was told to keep well away from the area, but I'm amazed to think now, how little interest I took in the whole event. I think most of the tidy-up operation would have taken place during school hours and my interest would have been rekindled when the builders started again.

Chapter Two – Gortan and Bowmore Schools

My seven years at our primary school at Gortan, one mile north of Bruichladdich, was an amazing experience. Built in the countryside, the single building was split in two with a single classroom to the left, and the resident teacher's house to the right. I only remember twelve to fourteen pupils, covering all seven years. The school had outside toilets, one male and one female. Boy, you had to be desperate to go on a winter's day. Get permission to leave the room, put your duffle coat on, walk about fifty yards to the toilet, and then freeze as the door wasn't exactly tight fitting. On the flip side, on a summer's day, going to the toilet was a good skive because for half the walk, you couldn't be seen from the classroom window. I'm sure Miss Campbell, our teacher, was well aware that we walked extremely slowly up past the gable end of the school, and we went to the toilet three times more frequently in the summer than winter.

Miss Campbell single handedly ran the school with all seven classes in a single classroom, a situation that would be unthinkable to teachers nowadays. Tish said that as a primary seven pupil, she'd be asked to help out with reading and writing with the younger pupils. It was truly amazing what one teacher achieved in such cramped conditions, but equally admirable was when she held the school Christmas party in her house. We had a great time and the highlight at the end of the afternoon was the prize giving ceremony. Nobody was left out and if you didn't get

Gortan Primary School.

Credit – Kent Rawlinson.

an award for certain subjects, you still received a book, and the sticker inside the front cover said 'For Merit'. What that meant was, you're not exceptional, but thanks for turning up.

I had three pupils in my class, myself, David McLachlan from the croft next door to our house, and Gwyneth Mitchell, the Distillery Exciseman's daughter.

Getting to school, a mile from the village was considerably safer in the 60s than nowadays. There was always something to see or do when going to school. The seals on the rocks sunbathing opposite Braeside and Loch Gorm houses, plenty of washed-up junk to check out as we walked on the shore and the Green Cross Code was never observed as we chased each other backwards and forwards across the road. Most us walked on the vast majority of schooldays. I can still remember the last thing Mum said, every morning without fail, was, 'Be careful on the road.' A lot of us had bikes and cycled to school when aged eleven or twelve, and we were anything but careful, but there was also a variety of passing vehicles that would stop, depending on how many were in a group. Alec McLellan's tractor and trailer was always popular. Five or six of us in the trailer wasn't uncommon.

Mr Mitchell, the Distillery Exciseman, had a fairly modern car. It could have been a Hillman Husky, certainly that shape and size. He would sometimes pick a couple of us up, but he insisted that all satchels had to be removed from our backs as he didn't want the metal buckles ripping his seats.

Of course, we all hero-worshipped the young men of the village and Gibson Campbell was one of them. Twice a week he used to take a tractor home from work at night, and next morning take a load of draff from the distillery to Tom Epps' farm at Gruinart for cattle feed. We never timed it right for a lift, he always seemed to pass the school at 9 am, just as the chosen pupil for the day rang the handbell to indicate classes were about to start. But we could all identify the sound of his tractor before he came round the corner. It was one of the first Massey Ferguson 135s on the island with 'Multi-power', probably the equivalent to overdrive in a car of that era. We were all fascinated by its speed. Steam used to billow from the trailer of hot draff straight out of Bruichladdich's mash tun and the smell was gorgeous.

I learned a hard-earned but never forgotten lesson one day, regarding a school class and an incident near our school. One Saturday early afternoon, Dad drove Mum, Norma and me to Bowmore for the weekly shopping. It was only nine miles to Bowmore, but a journey never without a talking point, including stopping our car in the car park at the top of the pier, and having our pet cat Blanche jump out of the engine compartment. Or Dad pulling up at the petrol pumps at Caskie's in Jamieson Street, getting out of the driving seat, and while he was in the shop, the car rolled merrily across the street with non-driver Mum screaming, 'How do you stop it?' and me, for once, the calm responsible nine-year-old pulling on the handbrake. So, back to the Saturday in question, about two hundred yards beyond Gortan School, a Caskie's tipper lorry (Caskie's was a Bowmore-based company, operating petrol pumps, a garage, shop, buses and lorries) had crashed into the hill face at the side of the road. The alternative, if it had crashed to the left side of the road instead of to the right, would have been a ten-foot drop into the sea. The lorry was still blocking part of the road as we drove past, and I just sat in the back seat, keeping quiet as always (be seen and not heard was always advisable), taking everything in, and listening intently. Too intently as it turned out. Anyway, Dad made a wee comment upon seeing the lorry, that he wouldn't be surprised if the driver had had a tipple or two. That was it, in my mind. I was in full receipt of the facts. In school on the Monday, Miss Campbell had a little discussion with all classes about lorries, the dangers of roads, and the incident. I put my hand up right away and said, 'Please Miss, I know what happened, my Dad said the driver was drunk.' Now, not only did I make a very rash statement in school, exaggerating Dad's thoughts, but at home, sitting at the dinner table at night, I stupidly told Mum and Dad the full story about how no-one knew the reason for the lorry crash, but I had put them all straight by telling them that my Dad knew the driver was drunk. I think by the end of the meal I had it drummed into me that I never ever was to repeat anything I heard like that in future.

But that didn't exactly stop me. Not terribly long after that, we went on holiday and firstly drove to the south west of Scotland. Dad wanted to visit Bladnoch Distillery, also owned by A.B. Grant, to see the manager, an old friend of his. We stayed the first night in a B&B guest house and in the living room was a quite hideous three-piece suite with faux leather backs and arms, and leopard-print cushions. As a family, we all went straight into the living room along with our host. As we sat down, there was an awkward silence and before the poor lady could offer us a cup of tea, I announced, 'Dad, this is one of these settees that you hate, isn't it?' Maybe that's why he just stopped telling me anything.

Other memories of Gortan include myself and Robin Currie (now Leader of Argyll and Bute Council) being sent to the spring, up the Kintraw road-end for fresh drinking water. It was a surface spring, at the side of the track, about fifty yards from the main road, and we'd take a couple of aluminium milk cans to fill.

Sports day was fun. We walked the few hundred yards to the Strand, the strip of land and beach along the northern edge of Lochindaal, separating the Rhinns from the 'other' side of the island from Bowmore to Port Ellen. Races were held on the flattest, grassiest, most sheep-dropping free bit we could find on the shore side of the road. I suppose we could be classed as semi-professional because there were monetary prizes. Threepence for the winner of each race, two old pennies for second place and a penny for third. To put that into perspective, Hastie's lemonade from Port Ellen came in two sizes of bottles, one shilling and twopence for the bigger size and 11d for the normal one.

Going back to the sports day, imagine the difficulty in holding fair races for a total of twelve boys and girls aged five to twelve. We were all very competitive but it must have been a nightmare for Miss Campbell to organise. The three-legged race, egg and spoon, and sack race were the only reasonably fair contests. The sacks used for the race were two hundredweight malt sacks from the distillery. They were huge and it felt like our wee legs could take two paces inside before the sack moved.

I'm sure our teacher, Miss Campbell, was glad of the one-hour break that she got in midweek when the music teacher from Bowmore School, followed by the PE teacher came to give her some respite. Miss Campbell went to her house for an hour while our visiting teachers spent time with us.

Music was always first and this was our first introduction to playing the recorder, but we had the craziest interaction with Mr McIlwraith, the PE teacher. Goodness only knows who started it, and it went on for years, but when the music teacher left, we all laid our heads in our arms on the desks and pretended to be asleep. Mr McIlwraith walked into the classroom and being so tall, he only seemed to take about three strides from the doorway to the desk. He went through the same procedure every week without raising his voice, and waited, sometimes several minutes till we lifted our heads and pretended we didn't know he'd arrived. As he walked towards the school each week, he must have thought, 'Here we go again with the crazy Gortan bunch,' but fair dues, he always humoured us.

In 1968, we made up a Gortan School five-a-side football team to take part in a tournament on the full-sized pitch at Port Charlotte. The pitch, which used to be in the countryside beyond

the village, is still there today, but now unrecognisable from the basic set of two goalposts in a field. The area now houses a community centre and campsite for visiting tents and camper vans. Until the tournament, we'd only ever played in Neil McLachlan's stackyard or the playground at the rear of Gortan School. This soon became obvious as I remember standing roughly in the middle of Port Charlotte pitch during our first match and the ball was kicked away towards the touchline. We all stopped playing because in our eyes, the ball was out. All the mums and dads started shouting and waving at us and we realised the ball was still in play, we just never dreamed that the edge of the pitch could be so far away. We won our age group in the tournament and qualified for the area finals in Campbeltown. We couldn't have been happier if you told us we were going to Hampden. However, fate dictated that I wasn't to realise my dream of playing in the finals, as you'll read later in Chapter Six that my appendix decided to play up on the same week as the finals. So I got to go to the mainland, but it was to the Western Infirmary in Glasgow via the ambulance plane and not to Campbeltown.

The School Concert at Christmas, held in Bruichladdich Hall, was a highlight. All the adults in the village turned up for that one so there was no hiding place. We spent months rehearsing and all of us would take part in two or three plays and sketches, as well as singing individually on stage. I remember one year having to learn the three verses and chorus of 'Song of the Clyde' which are quite long and daunting for a ten-year-old. Unfortunately, this included having to recite Kenneth McKellar's 'optional' third verse, sometimes referred to as the 'patter' verse. It's got lots more words per line and sung at breakneck speed. If you know the tune, have a go at singing it:

There's Paw an' Maw doon at the Broomielaw,
They're goin' doon the watter for the Fair;
There's Bob an' Mary on the Govan Ferry,
Wishin' jet propulsion could be there;
There's steamers cruisin', and there's buddies snoozin',
And there's laddies fishin' frae the pier;
An' Paw's perspirin', very near expirin',
As he rows a boat frae there to here;
With eyes a-flashin', it is voted smashin',

To be walkin' daily on the prom;
And May and Evelyn are in seventh heaven,
As they stroll along with Dick and Tom;
And Dumbarton Rock to ev'ry Jean and Jock,
Extends a welcome that is high and wide;
Seems to know that they are on their homeward way,
To hear the song of the Clyde.

One thing I was involved in, and loved, was going round the village on behalf of the school with a collection tin on a Saturday morning with Allistair Learmond, looking for contributions to various important charities. We were always trying to beat the money raised from previous collections and because we got the collecting tins home with us on a Friday, we deliberately walked past the distillery workers heading home with their wage packets, and they quite often gave us some coins. Also, anyone in the village that we knew would be out at work on a Saturday got a visit at Friday teatime. Typically in a year, maybe three times, collections were held for Poppy Day, Red Cross and the Children's Home at Rhu (Helensburgh). Unlike nowadays where people don't appreciate 'cold callers', most people in the village knew when the collections were expected and welcomed us. There were various sweets and drinks offered to sustain us, as I suppose people appreciated us coming, and also recognised it was quite a task. By the time we'd trekked through the whole village along the shoreline, up to Conisby, past all the distillery cottages, through Burnside, we were both pretty tired. However, there was a wee bit of method in our madness too, because ending up at Burnside, we both knew that there was one more little walk, up the hill to the farm at Gartacharra. There, Mrs McGregor would invite us in for a cup of tea and a girdle scone. You've never tasted such a welcome treat and of course she knew that two growing boys would never refuse seconds.

I wonder if any ex-Gortan pupils remember a weird bad habit we all developed when asking questions. Actually, Miss Campbell addressed the whole school one day to see where it started, who started it, and how we thought we could avoid it. None of us were even aware until she highlighted it to us, but looking back now, I find it amazing how a whole bunch of kids would copy each other without a second thought. The habit was putting 'I don't know' at the start of every question. So when it was playtime, loads of kids wanted to ask the teacher a question. So she'd be inundated with:

'Please Miss, I don't know, can we go out and play?'

'Please Miss, I don't know, is it all right if I draw on the blackboard?'

'Please Miss, I don't know, do you know what happened in the playground yesterday?'

'Please Miss, I don't know, do you want to taste one of my sweets?'

Strange that we never did it at home, and the habit never followed us to school in Bowmore, but Miss Campbell's patience must have paid off because I don't remember it being mentioned when she retired and when my younger sister, Norma, attended Gortan School under new teacher Mrs McIlwraith.

On the back wall that divided the classroom from the eating area, we always had a huge drawing to do on a frieze as a project for the whole school. I imagine it was usually about ten feet long and about six feet high. It was filled in over the course of a few months and each class did their bit depending on ability. One year we drew the classic Chinese 'Willow Pattern' plate design. I had to start it off on the blank paper which was quite daunting, and I'm no artist.

Another project that sticks in my mind was, as a practical test, the boys all had to make a puffer from wood. We were given a 4in x 4in piece of wood and had to carve the bow and stern to make the hull. We used penknives, no vice to hold the wood, just holding it at our desks, and thinking of it now, it's a blessing no-one cut themselves.

We used to get one lesson a week on an educational schools radio channel. Once we were all encouraged to make a flat roof house from a shoebox, then using matchboxes, form a staircase up one end of it. The staircase took about twelve matchboxes each, multiplied by about a dozen pupils so you can imagine the scramble for matchboxes in the village. No-one and no house was exempt from being pestered by us in our pursuit and of course everyone wanted to finish first.

When I left Gortan and moved up to the High School in Bowmore, three of us, myself and two from Port Ellen side were still made to wear short trousers by our parents. This didn't do a lot for my street cred, but can you imagine my sheer delight when, after three months of enduring cold legs and teasing, during the Tattie Holidays in October, Mum and Dad relented and bought me long trousers and elastic-sided shoes. Oh my God, elastic-sided shoes, I spent the entire holiday just looking at them. I'm not saying I led a very sheltered life (much), but I was now a fashion icon in my own eyes.

It was a nine-mile drive to Bowmore School in a Caskie's bus, starting from Portnahaven and picking us up en route. Two buses came from the Port Ellen end of the island, and another, Donald Bell's bus, from Port Askaig. I used to sit with MacBrayne's Pier Master's son Alan MacDiarmid (Quackers) from Port Charlotte and there was always good banter all around. Most of the laughs came from our resident comedian John McLellan, who later went on to become legendary manager of Bunnahabhain Distillery. John sat at the seat beside the door (no self-opening doors in these days), and opened the door at each stop. No-one got past him without at least some comment, or he'd give you a gentle shove at the top of the steps to encourage you to leave the bus quicker.

At Bowmore School I learned a valuable lesson in listening properly, and never assuming anything. At the end-of-year prize-giving in fourth year, I nearly made a fool of myself. Because we lived on an island, we had the opportunity to take Navigation as a subject instead of woodwork. I was always top of the class and in third year I got about 80 per cent in my final exams and in fourth year I got 90 per cent. So it came to the prize-giving ceremony and the Headmaster stated that he was now going to award a new special prize for Navigation, which was a cup donated by Mrs Beaton in memory of her late husband who was a bank manager in Bowmore. He announced, 'The winner for the most improved student in Navigation is …' At this point I very nearly stood up. I can't remember who won but someone, to my horror, had raised his results from 30 per cent to 50 per cent, therefore he was the most improved. I must listen more intently in future to the wording.

Chapter Three – Playing in the Distillery

In modern times, and quite rightly so, workplaces are not advisable for children to play in, but in the 60s, we had a bit of a free hand and could certainly hang about in the yard or even venture into buildings on malt intake days. The production areas were really the only places we knew to keep away from. The distillery yard was a convenient shortcut when I cycled from Burnside to our house, but it would always take me three times longer to get home because there was always something going on, and the workers always made time for me.

Bruichladdich Distillery staff on one of Miss Thomson's visits.

Credit – Family photo.

Bruichladdich Distillery had a unique layout with practically everything happening within the enclosed yard. I loved the sound of empty casks bouncing on the concrete as they were being pushed across the yard from the Cooperage to the Filling Store ready for the next morning's filling. There was so much to see if the filling store was in operation. Men hammering in the bungs on casks, others shouting out the weight of each cask for someone in the filling store office to calculate the gallons of spirit, and the air was full of the gorgeous smell of the new make spirit. After the filling, the men had to load the lorries by pushing the full casks up a portable wooden ramp, or 'skids' as they were known, and then when the trailer was full, they were taken to the warehouses either at Burnside or up the Conisby road. We got to sit on the casks on the flatbed trailers which was great fun. Unfortunately, that came to a stop when one day (I was at school so never saw it) the lorry had to change gear going up the Burnside brae and the jolt caused a cask to fall off the back of a lorry, breaking a man's ankle. As a result, all open back lorries in future reversed up the hill so the cab supported the casks, and youngsters never got to hitch a lift.

So the malt came by puffers (small coastal cargo boats), into Bruichladdich pier, and was transported in two-hundredweight hessian sacks. The Distillery had two long flat-bed lorries, a green Albion and a red Thames Trader. Ronnie Learmond, the Distillery Joiner, and Ian MacKinnon, Engineer, were the drivers for the day. HGV licences weren't introduced until February 1970 so Dad would sometimes have a shot at moving a lorry, or maybe just drive it in the village or up to the warehouses at Burnside. Well, the less said about his driving skills, the better. I'm certainly grateful that he never had the opportunity to drive a lorry onto the pier, that would have been scary. Usually a couple of local men, often crofters, were employed temporarily to work in the hold of the boat. Bags were lifted, four at a time, onto the lorries which, when fully loaded, were driven the short distance to the malt intake in the Distillery yard. Each lorry would allow one boy as a passenger for the day and even though each load was exactly the same routine, and the distance from the end of the pier to the malt intake was probably five hundred yards, we were never bored for a second. If you wanted to get a seat in the lorry, you had to be out early, so I suppose living in the Distillery grounds and having inside information that a puffer was arriving through the night, helped. I always wanted to go in the Thames Trader with Ronnie, an absolutely iconically designed lorry. Unfortunately, the lorries hardly had time to get out of second gear, the journey was so short, but sitting so high up, going through the village, we felt so important.

Thames Trader lorry loading full casks onto puffer.

Credit – Family photo.

At the pier we were allowed out of the cab and took any opportunity to jump onto the puffer. Some skippers chased us, but the majority of the crews were fine. Unfortunately, our house front window looked directly across at the pier and I'm sure Mum watched me like a hawk. Of course, as a parent and grandparent now I fully understand her anxiety as lorries, boats, and bags of malt swinging over our heads aren't exactly the ideal safe playgrounds for children, but we thought we were invincible. So when the lorry reversed up to the boat, it hid the view from the house and I could jump onto the puffer. The secret was to jump when the heavy bags, slung by the boat's derrick and winch, were over the lorry, as that meant the boat was leaning towards the pier so a much shorter leap. I loved watching the men in the hold. Such hard manual labour, but when the lorry was sitting, waiting on the pier, there was no rest for them.

Bruichladdich Distillery from the pier. Our house to the right of the white distillery buildings.

Credit – Whisky.com

Back at the Distillery, we helped push the bags of malt on a sack-barrow from the trailer into the malt intake chute. Other times we carried the empty bags away from the intake to keep the area clear. The lorry driver's first job was to cut the string on top of each bag and that was one thing we were never allowed to do. Boys and knives, working on top of a trailer, would have been a perfect recipe for disaster. Recycling is such a buzz word nowadays but we also played our part in the 60s. The empty hessian sacks were rolled up and stuffed inside sacks for transporting back to the mainland. I used to love watching the men sewing the bags closed with string and an enormous curved needle. We'd sit on top of the sacks and they'd tell me all sorts of stories, some of which I'm sure were far-fetched, but I always listened intently.

We took great interest in the puffers and if we saw one in the mouth of Lochindaal, we'd immediately try to identify them in the distance by their slightly different shapes. Then we'd run to the pier and feel really important when we got to catch the ropes thrown by the crew, and throw them over the bollards. The *Lady Isle*, *Limelight*, *Raylight*, *Moonlight*, *Dawnlight* and *Stormlight* were the most regular puffers to visit. Little did we know that within a decade, their work here would no longer be required.

It was very interesting reading through the websites of old shipping companies while researching some dates for this book, and seeing the fate of some of the boats. There are some particularly sad photos of puffers torn apart in breakers yards. The end of the *Limelight* was well known to us all. She perished on the rocks at Port Ellen when arriving with building materials. I remember seeing her from the *Lochiel* as we sailed past, still partially above water, looking so sad and helpless. The *Raylight* sank in 1975 off Larne, north of Belfast.

The *Stormlight* ran aground near Craighouse on Jura in 1973 and was declared a wreck.

M.V. Dawnlight.

Credit – Scottish Maritime Museum.

M.V. Moonlight.

Credit – Rod Lightbody.

The *Dawnlight* was luckier, she changed hands several times within the UK, at one time serving the Island of Lundy in the Bristol Channel, then was renamed *Agnes* and in 2010 she was still working in Honduras. It's coincidental how several boats have moved on and had been stationed very close to where I now live between Bath and Bristol. Not only the *Dawnlight* plying her trade here in the Bristol Channel for a few years, but also the *Lochiel* ended her life as a floating restaurant in Bristol Dockside from 1978 till her scrapping in 1995. She was branded the *Inn at the Quay* and painted with a red hull and white upper structure.

Lochiel in her latter days as a restaurant 'Inn at the Quay' in Bristol Dockside.

Credit – Mark Winter.

Other areas of the Distillery we could visit were sheds, empty cask store, cooperage, draff bay, coal yard and underneath the malt bins. As long as we kept out of the production areas we were usually left to our own devices. There was a three-sided shed area, known as the tunnel (beside the current bottling hall) and it was the access between our house and the Distillery. It was a storage area for the Distillery, but an adventure ground for youngsters and made a great play area on wet days. Wood was stacked in one corner, cement blocks in another so to a young mind, that can only mean building ramps for us to play on our bikes. Don't get me wrong, Dad hadn't gone soft, he probably regarded us as little vermin but if we weren't messing about too much, we'd be tolerated.

On the seashore in front of the Distillery, the pot ale (residue from wash stills) pipe stretched out into the sea. I can only estimate it must have been about eighteen inches in diameter because it was fairly easy for us to walk on. It was designed to always be submerged, or at least for the outlet to be under water as much as possible, but occasionally at a very low tide we could virtually walk to the end. In most weather and tidal conditions we certainly could walk some way along the top of the pipe. Luckily, the Distillery buildings obscured Mum's view of the pipe from our front window because she'd probably have had kittens if she'd seen her wee boy wandering out to sea. We never had any way of knowing when pot ale would be discharged into the sea but if we were lucky enough to be on the shore when it happened, we would often be treated to a spectacular display of mullet splashing about, obviously delighted that it was feeding time. We never tried to catch them by line or net, just happy to observe such big fish around our feet. Mullet were regarded as scavengers and rarely caught. This was evidence that pot ale wasn't, and isn't, harmful, but nowadays it is taken away by road tankers and discharged in faster flowing water in the Sound of Islay, just south of Caol Ila Distillery.

Again, as I've mentioned elsewhere in the book, it was surprising that we were never encouraged to learn to swim as it was quite dangerous balancing on a round cast iron pipe which could be slippery in places with seaweed on it as the tide receded.

I did have one advantage because of who I was, and that was being allowed to go as passenger in Clyne's lorry delivering draff to local farms if it was a weekend or outside school hours. If I was on time, I'd get into the mash house to watch the draff being transferred from the mash tun to the lorry. The lorry was parked directly below the mash tun and two workers shovelled the draff down two chutes. It was ridiculously hot and hard work, but also comical because the mashman would mark a line on the draff with his shovel across the diameter of the mash tun. So each man knew his half of the draff to shovel and no way was he going to encroach into the other one's half. Down below, after some of the draff was in the trailer, it was necessary to use a long-handled scraper to spread the draff across the lorry. I loved jumping up on the back wheels and pushing and pulling draff into the corners of the trailer. It was really hot work, often you couldn't see the draff for the steam, and I used to think I was being really helpful. Well, I was, because Engy, the driver, was quite content, leaning against a wall, watching from a safe distance, smoking his fag, and barking instructions to me. We'd usually deliver to Coull, Craigens, Kilchiaran and Gearach farms. Coull was always on a Saturday morning, and my favourite was Craigens on a Friday evening. It was quite scary on the single track roads on a winter's evening as the lorry headlights were nothing like as efficient as today's vehicles.

When I think of Gearach and the draff lorry, I do have minor flashbacks of the day I nearly lost a finger. I didn't ever dare to tell Dad this story as I'd never have been allowed in the lorry again, but the routine always was that I would jump out of the cab and as the trailer started to tip, I'd open the back door. Unfortunately, on this one occasion, I thought I'd be clever and push the holding pin out with my finger, only for my finger to take its place holding the door shut. Luckily, I was seen in the lorry mirror, jumping about like an idiot to grab attention. That was certainly a finger that needed running under a cold tap, and luckily there was a cow's water trough nearby.

Another use of the contractor's draff lorry was for coal deliveries. During the week, it would deliver single bags to houses locally, but Saturday morning was the big run to Bowmore. The lorry was loaded up with hundredweight bags, three high, on Friday afternoon. I was twelve years old and could just about drag a bag of coal across the trailer. A run to Bowmore was just the best and I never knew there were so many houses, as all I'd ever seen was the shops, the football pitch and the school. Two men carried the bags, and I positioned the bags on the edge of the trailer for them to carry, high on their shoulders. Sometimes, the men would disappear into a customer's house for literally two minutes. I used to think, 'That was a quick cuppa' but I reckon now of course that a dram was more likely the reason.

One big attraction was playing around the distillery yard in the summer holidays when Rankins were building warehouses. Often there would be workers from the mainland, usually mixing cement, and we were just fascinated by them and their stories. One thing we loved doing was running errands for the workers to MacLeod's shop in the village, and a typical order would be two bottles of lemonade, bars of chocolate and 20 Embassy tipped cigarettes. Yes, purchasing cigarettes was never an issue, even for ten-year-olds, and we were never even questioned as to who they were for. We'd also normally take back the empty lemonade bottles from the day before, and we'd get to keep the return money. There was no better feeling than going round the building site of a half-finished warehouse and finding empty lemonade bottles. It was a case of finders, keepers, and often we'd go back to the shop in an evening with an armful of empties.

For me, a sign of the times came in 1968 when the new Western Ferries company introduced their *Sound of Islay* roll-on/roll-off ferry from the mainland. This was a totally new concept, offering something that MacBrayne's mail boats, MacBrayne's cargo boats, and the Light Company's puffers couldn't, and that was lorries driving straight on and off the boats. Bruichladdich Distillery was involved in several of the first sailings. Previous to the *Sound of Islay* being introduced, in 1966 Eileann Sea Services started a landing craft type boat service to Port Ellen. The boat could carry four lorries, roll-on/roll-off, or the equivalent in cars. There was a lot of dubiety about the safety and comfort of such a vessel in open water. I remember we went on holiday to Forres and Dad took the car on the landing craft *Isle of Gigha* but he insisted the rest of the family flew to Campbeltown and he'd pick us up. Everyone's fears were realised in November 1966 when the *Isle of Gigha* capsized en route to Islay and one of the lorries on board was carrying a load of steel racking for Bruichladdich's latest warehouse. The lorries were condemned to the bottom of the sea and unfortunately three men lost their lives in the incident. The *Isle of Gigha* was salvaged and renamed *Sound of Gigha* in 1969. She was modified and introduced to the Port Askaig to Jura service in 1969.

Happier memories though, were of articulated lorries coming to Bruichladdich Distillery for the first time. I remember one dark evening, Dad said, 'Come and see something you'll like.' Of course, I was out like a shot but he wouldn't tell me what we were waiting for. We stood in front of the Distillery and a set of what seemed like huge headlights appeared from the direction of the village hall. As a twelve-year-old, I think I must have been standing open-mouthed, in awe of what I saw. The only recollection I had of an articulated lorry was on holiday on the mainland, seeing small versions being operated by British Rail (or whatever the rail operator was called in those days) at their stations. In fact, the lorry units were three-wheelers so that's how small they were. But now, pulling up in front of us was Bruichladdich's first delivery of bulk malt in a Kelman of Turriff articulated lorry. To me, it was enormous (probably tiny by today's standards) but looked magnificent in its red and green company colours. It was quite an operation manoeuvring it through the front gates and I stayed and watched the whole unloading procedure. I'm sure I must have seen the construction of the new ground level malt intake but it never registered in my brain that such a change was about to take place. No doubt when the malt intake hopper and plinth were being made, I was probably more interested in collecting the workers' empty lemonade bottles to boost my pocket money.

Kelman of Turriff malt lorry.

Credit – Turriff Heritage Society.

The next revelation was the movement of empty and full casks by road. I didn't realise it at the time but in all the fascination of those majestic articulated lorries, I'd actually witnessed the demise of the puffers overnight. The first delivery of casks to Bruichladdich was by Dobson's of Edinburgh and I recall the two green Atkinson lorries arriving together. Two impeccably loaded trailers of newly coopered casks three high, all unloaded into the Distillery yard. Then unexpectedly, to me anyway, both lorries were immediately loaded with full casks. With the bottom row of casks standing up on their ends, three wide, a second tier, two casks wide, was rolled on top.

I'm sure today that His Majesty's Revenue and Customs would have reservations about this being loaded onto an open flat-bed trailer with just a net holding the casks in place. But that's how it was done, and the icing on the cake to this tale was that I was offered the chance to go as passenger on the first of the two lorries to the ferry at Port Askaig. Words failed me at the time, I just couldn't take it all in, and although it was a privilege to have been on one of the first articulated lorries on Islay, only now do I realise the impact it must have made on the puffer companies and employees seeing their livelihood disappear in a very short time.

Dobson of Edinburgh lorry with casks. Dobson worked predominantly with Scottish & Newcastle Brewers before involvement with whisky.

Credit – Heineken Brewers.

We had a garage built between the two warehouses behind our house. When Tish was old enough to drive, Dad had the garage extended to accommodate two cars, one behind the other. Of course, to everyone else this is now a big long garage, but to a young boy, it's now a five-a-side indoor football pitch. Often, on a rainy day, a couple of friends and I would have a kick about inside the garage, but one afternoon I was on my own, booting the ball against the back wall. Now I have got eyes, I really did notice that there was a window, and all my shots were low and accurate. However, I got more adventurous and the shots got harder and more wayward. Inevitably, one went right through the new pane of glass. I thought, 'Here goes, another roasting.' But no, this time I had a master plan, so I went outside and found a slate. I placed it on the floor inside the garage directly below the window. A day or two later, Dad and I went into the garage and I acted nonchalantly, looking everywhere except in the direction of the back wall. It took a few minutes for him to notice the broken pane of glass and he came out with a cruder version of, 'Oh dear, the window appears to be broken.'

I pretended not to hear but ambled towards him and then acting totally surprised, I said, 'Look Dad, a slate, it's come off the warehouse roof, that's what'll have done it.' I may as well have said 'Guilty'. Dad, raging, but probably trying not to grin said, 'How's that, when all the warehouses have tin roofs.' Then just to rub it in, he said, 'Why's all the glass outside, and the slate is inside?' Oh well, another few days in the doghouse.

Obviously with my Dad as Manager, I got opportunities to enter production areas periodically with him. The Engineer's workshop was in a dark corner of the Lower Stillhouse. I recall the smell of oils and greases and the benches were covered in dismantled parts of machinery. I adore all smells in distillery production, yeast, spirit, pot ale, draff, washbacks etc., and I'm sure it comes from being around them as a youngster. Nowadays, some distilleries are so clinical with more sealed vessels, no filling stores or warehouses, and there aren't the smells, and there most certainly isn't the character and atmosphere of days gone by. Smells in the Stillhouse were slightly more overpowering for a youngster but I loved the atmosphere.

Sometimes in an evening, Dad would take me to the Stillhouse to watch him reduce (adding water to make every batch an exact cask filling strength) the spirit. This involved the Manager, Exciseman and Stillman to be present. I loved the routine they all had. The Stillman taking countless samples and Dad crouching down to the height of the sampling glass to read the hydrometer. Exciseman Jim Mitchell was peering over Dad's shoulder, and then when they flicked through the alcohol table books and scribbled figures with chalk on a small black board, they'd shout out a quantity of water to the stillman. This was the signal to fill copper measuring jugs with an exact amount of cold water and add it to the spirit vessel. It was heavy work but I was allowed to empty the smaller jugs. Then the Stillman would rummage (stir) the water and spirit with a long wooden pole and paddle so that a more accurate reading could be taken of the new strength. The present-day equivalent involves fewer people in the task, electric stirrers in the vessel, calculators, water batch meters and job done in a quarter of the time. More efficient – Yes. More enjoyable working atmosphere today - definitely No.

For me as a youngster, the Tun room didn't hold much interest, it was really the route we walked from the Stillhouse to the Mash House. Maybe if yeast was being added, or the men were inside a washback cleaning with a heather broom, I'd stop and watch, otherwise I'd just enjoy stamping my feet on the noisy steel floor grating.

In the Mash House, the mash tun was spectacular. The large stirrer rotated like huge claws, and was supported round the circumference of the vessel by serrated teeth. Absolutely no protection to anyone standing around the vessel but everyone was just aware that it was an open topped vessel, extremely dangerous and as a child I couldn't be watched all the time. There were surprisingly few accidents considering the nature of the industry. I'm a hundred per cent in favour of Health and Safety and have been a Trade Union Health and Safety Shop Steward in my latter years, but in the Sixties, everyone used common sense and awareness to keep themselves safe. Safety is paramount nowadays with the suing culture everywhere, but I feel H&S sometimes makes people less likely to use common sense.

Bruichladdich Distillery Mash Tun

Credit – Joe Collver.

One thing I used to think was really grown-up was just before the distillery day workers went home at 5 pm, they all lined up outside the office to get their dram and I'd get to stand and watch. Dad would produce a little horn cup and each man in turn would get their last dram of the working day. Because it was time for everyone to go home, the mood was good and there were lots of laughs. Some men would take the plastic cup from the top of their flask and get the dram poured into that so that they could sip it a bit more slowly but I used to love watching the older guys who would throw the dram down their neck, then screw their face up as though they'd eaten an onion, and then they'd say, 'Christ that was good.' It was amazing how every lorry driver on the island seemed to be passing, or finished unloading a lorry at a distillery at exactly 4.55 pm every evening, and then when asked if they wanted to join the queue for a dram, they would act totally surprised.

A final Distillery tale from the late 60s was when Hamish McDonald came to Islay to be Dad's Brewer (Assistant Manager) at Bruichladdich. Hamish had (and still has, I spoke to him in 2022) a really broad North of Scotland accent and even those of us who've spent years on Speyside have to concentrate sometimes on some of his Doric phrases, so Islay men certainly weren't used to his accent and speed of talking. One day Dad was standing at the top of the office stairs, directly above the filling store. He was leaning on the handrail surveying everything that was happening in the Distillery yard. He saw Hamish talking to one of the Distillery labourers and the guy was listening intently. Dad had already asked Hamish to give the worker a job to do. After the conversation, Hamish and the Distillery worker went off in different directions. Dad knew the worker was going the wrong way, bearing in mind the instructions he had given Hamish, and Dad was going down the stairs anyway, so he thought he'd meet the worker at the bottom of the stairs to see where he was going. 'You're not supposed to be over here,' Dad said, 'What did Hamish just tell you to do?' 'I haven't got a clue, Mr Logie,' he replied, 'So I thought I'd come and see you.'

Chapter Four – What Kids Did

Halloween was a much-loved night and all the children in the village played a big part in its success. Many evenings were spent preparing costumes during the previous week to ensure that everyone looked their best, and more importantly, wouldn't be recognised. There was a bit of competition amongst the children to be best dressed before we ever got out to the houses.

First priority, in the days before carrier bags, was ensuring you had a good-sized strong shopping bag because you were assured a good haul of monkey nuts, sweets, tablet, toffee apples (if you were lucky), fruit and money throughout the evening. Secondly, timing was critical. We always waited till it was properly dark, tried to ensure we weren't first ones on the circuit, but also were very aware that to get the best pickings, being last out wasn't exactly ideal. Once out, we knew that sticking to groups of two, three or maximum of four was best. Bigger groups wouldn't be so flexible to go to houses that everyone could agree on, and really big groups didn't get invited into houses, which was the best way to get the rich pickings. Most of us rehearsed a quick rhyme or joke to recite in each house if asked, and although we were never Americanised enough to call it Trick or Treat, it was all about getting identified quickly, doing our little party piece and moving on to the next house. Anyway, we could never shout 'Trick or Treat' because being such a small village, everyone knew our voices and our disguise would have been blown.

Of course, strategy came into our Halloween plans. There were some seriously rich pickings to be had, and often, the best ones were in reasonably short supply. Dorothy McEachern's toffee apples were a must. Mrs Kirk's treacle toffees were legendary. So, we're already talking about Dorothy's near the pier, and Mrs Kirk was the last house in Burnside, so two extremities of the village, so brisk walking was called for. A breezy evening, coupled with wearing clumsy outfits, made running difficult but this was serious competition for food.

Then there were the tactics of not telling anyone else where the goodies were, and it was known for 'rival' groups from Burnside and from the bottom of the village to deviate each other away from the attractive hauls by promising each other that there were fantastic selections to be had at a certain house. Obviously, nobody was in that house on that evening so after being fooled, and knowing the 'best' houses were running short, the tactics and the mood changed, everything became fair in love and war, and we all started going round each house in the village in order, with each group not keeping too close to the next one. It was a known fact that if too many kids appeared on a doorstep at one time, the share of sweets etc. was smaller, and also another very important observation for a food lover like myself was that men's hands were bigger so if a couple were both involved in putting something in our bags, you got a bigger handful of monkey nuts from the man of the house.

I do remember on a couple of years, an adult dressed entirely in black, with a mask, used to stand at the top of the hill, just beyond the Distillery back gate. He (I think it was a man) never moved, never spoke, and scared the living daylights out of us. Street lighting wasn't great in the village and even when we came down the hill and got to the main road, we turned to look and he never budged. Obviously a great costume and I hope it was done to join in the atmosphere of the evening, but by God, it was scary to a nine-or ten-year-old.

Bonfire Night, held on the Saturday closest to November 5th, was a great community effort. The bonfire was erected on the flattest surface on 'Tait's Rocks' on the seashore directly in front of Dr Tait's house. In the early 60s Dr Tait ran his surgery from a room in his house before having a purpose-built surgery built in the front garden. I never knew who named the rocks but it's a beautiful testimony to a wonderful man.

The most amazing thing about the bonfire was that for the weekend and week prior to the event, the local children used to collect all the materials for the fire. Nobody prompted us, nobody even fixed a date to start, but most houses had a barrow-full of stuff looked out ready for us, and we didn't discuss it amongst ourselves, it just happened. I remember borrowing a couple of sack barrows from the Distillery and we literally went round every house in the village and collected everyone's contribution. Bundles of old newspapers, wooden crates, cardboard boxes and wood from gardens (pallets weren't readily available then) were the most popular items with the odd small pieces of furniture. Some days were tiring, especially walking as far as Mrs Gillespie's on the southern outskirts of the village.

As children, we were pretty damn good at building a safe bonfire, but on the Saturday morning of Bonfire Night, the Distillery lorry would come over with some decent materials and the men would put the finishing touches and make sure the bonfire was safe and steady. The Distillery provided some large pieces of wood, boxes and small damaged ex-yeast barrels which helped the bonfire burn well into the night. On the night, we took no part in the organisation, we'd done our bit and the adults took over the lighting of the fire and fireworks.

Christmas in Bruichladdich meant excitement at the annual children's Christmas party in the village hall. There were lots of games; Grand Old Duke of York for example was popular. Pass the parcel was a bit chaotic as you didn't know whether to pass the parcel slowly because it would be in your hands for longer, or pass it quickly and hope it came round to you again. Musical chairs became a bit physical when it came down to the last three or four still in the game. Bee Baw Babbity was a strange game. Everyone firstly stood in a big circle, boy, girl, boy, girl, round the hall with a boy standing in the middle. We all held hands and slowly walked clockwise singing:

Bee Baw Babbity, Babbity, Babbity,
Bee Baw Babbity, kiss a bonnie wee lassie,
You wouldnae hae a laddie-o, a laddie-o, a laddie-o,
You wouldnae hae a laddie-o, now kiss a bonnie wee lassie.

Then we'd stop going round, the boy in the middle had to kiss a girl on the cheek and she'd replace him in the centre. For the shy ones like me, tapping a girl on the shoulder was sufficient. Then the whole thing repeated with 'Lassie' replacing 'Laddie', and vice-versa in the song.

There was always lovely grub at the party, and plenty of it, and then the finale, Santa. Now only a few years ago, my Mum started dropping cryptic clues about Santa, and got me thinking that after all these years, it was my Dad all the time. I don't suppose I took a vast interest in Santa's height or build; the bag of presents was way more important. And anyway now, I don't really think I want to know who it was. That last sentence will guarantee that someone will tell me now, so thank you in advance.

Christmas Eve evening was usually a drive to St Kiaran's Church, between Bruichladdich and Port Charlotte, for a service. It was always expected of Distillery Managers to hold some sort of office outside their day-to-day role, so Dad was an Elder of the Church and Treasurer for a while and therefore we regularly attended. But it was what was promised to me that made the evening bearable. In return for me (my sisters were probably the same) attending and not moaning, we got to open one present when we got home. Most years we picked Auntie Betty's present from Saskatchewan in Canada. The brown-paper-wrapped parcel used to sit for days under the Christmas tree with the customs label telling us exactly what was inside. Just the fact sweets were called candies made them taste ten times better than UK versions.

Christmas Day in a Dorran in Bruichladdich wasn't hugely different to a lot of other days once the presents were opened. I was easily pleased, new football, new football boots, and straight out to play. One other present we were always guaranteed was a pocket diary. Later on Christmas Day I'd meticulously fill in the name, address, and telephone number page at the front, mark down my own birthday for some reason, then never look at the diary ever again for the whole year. I'm always reminded of Christmas Dinner by one photo we have at home. I had to wear a tie, under protest, and also, I think I'm still traumatised by the loud 60s wallpaper in the dining room.

However, New Year's Day was a bit special. Living in the Manager's house meant not having to go out because all the distillery workers who lived in the village took it in turn to 'first foot' us. Time for another childish master plan. So after lunch (when I actually got a glass of cider with my meal), as each of the men called round, there were tins of shortbread on the coffee table, so fair game for me to pick away at. Dad would give each of the men a dram, then they'd produce a half-bottle from the inside pocket of their jacket to return the compliment. Best tactic was to stand beside the men and really try to get into the conversation, then as the day went on, the men got more and more tipsy and jokingly said to me, 'Are you for a dram?' Dad would say, 'No no, he can have some of this cider,' and I'd end up with another glass. It's funny how drinking in the house was so formal, and everyone had their own drink that they stuck to. Dad, a great believer in having, as he said, 'a good splash of water' in his whisky, stuck to his drams of Royal Scot blended whisky. I was getting giggly with all the cider I was being offered, and poor Mum must have had Advocaat coming out of her ears by the end of the day. We were always told that at that time, Bruichladdich Malt Whisky was a substantial component of the Royal Scot blend.

Having mentioned that Dad served as Church Treasurer for a while reminds me of a little job we used to do regularly as a family after regular Sunday evening services. Kilchoman Church was part of the same Parish and in summer evenings we'd drive there to collect some money from a collection point. This is one of the many things in life that I annoyingly never asked about at the time. Round the back of the Church, amongst the gravestones, there was a stone plinth with a hole, not much bigger than your fist, sunk into it. It had a small rounded, sort of bell-shaped stone covering it, and every week the hole, as well as having rain water in it, was full of loose change. I never ever worked out why anyone knew this was a collection point but I used to love running ahead and getting the coins out. There was something magical about seeing the coins sitting glistening in clean rainwater under the setting sun.

Surprisingly, although there were a lot of children in the village, there weren't an awful lot of birthday parties to attend. It just wasn't really the done thing to gather all the kids together. There was an exception, and that was at Jim and Nan Mitchell's for Gwyneth's birthdays. As you'd by now expect me to say, the party food was exceptional. They had a lovely big Distillery House, lots of rooms for a dozen or so children to play games. As we got older, they introduced a version of Postman Knock. Crikey, I don't know how the girls felt, I was petrified.

Mrs Mitchell also held Beetle Drives in their house (throw a dice, each number represents a beetle body part, first one to complete the body, wins. Six was the body, a five for the head, four for each of the two wings, threes had to be thrown for each of the six legs, twos entitled you to attach each of the two antenna, and a couple of ones on the dice got you both eyes). They were probably raising money for the WRI or suchlike. I think they got about four tables of four people in the back room. Mind you, not your average game where you drew a beetle on a scorecard, these were plastic model beetles to make up.

I refer a few times to how village life was wonderful but I was certainly not the most worldly-wise child. For some reason, we were in Morayshire, on holiday maybe, I was about nine, and Dad took me to the cinema for the first time. Bizarrely, I was wearing my kilt, and no-one ever told me that cinema seats weren't just chairs, but they were hinged and had to be held down. So of course, in the dark, I sat on what I thought was the seat but it was in the upright position. I was now head and shoulders above everyone else. So Dad explained that I had to hold the seat down, so I did that, and then I straightened my kilt and the seat sprung up again. This went on two or three times till eventually the seat was held for me. To make matters worse, I asked to go to the toilets after about an hour, and off I went on my own. Again, struggling in the dark, I saw a door which had the word 'Exit'. How was I supposed to know that had I read it properly, it actually said 'Fire Exit'. So now, I'm a little boy, standing in Elgin High Street on a busy Saturday afternoon, with the door closed behind me. I can only imagine the panic inside when it was clear that I'd got seriously lost. Who thought a simple thing like the cinema could turn into an adventure.

I used to attend Lifeboys meetings one evening a week in Port Charlotte school. Mrs Frew, PE teacher (or PT teachers as they were known then) at Bowmore School was in charge. Lifeboys were seen as a stepping stone to the Boys' Brigade, but originated as a religious meeting place for boys affiliated to a Church or Sunday School. Misleadingly, we all wore Navy-style hats and jumpers with various lanyards, so it was easy to think of us as a nautical organisation, rather than the original intended character-building groups. Suffice to say we never went in a boat or saw the sea during our evening meetings, but any time we were asked what we wanted to do, immediately 'Football' was the cry. In inclement weather, we stayed indoors and a lot of activities were team-based sports like skittles, softball etc. There was a structure for all Lifeboys groups around the country. We were divided into three teams and, in Port Charlotte, we decided to be named after football teams, Hibs, Rangers and Celtic. I was team leader in Hibs, and how I hated not being quick enough to shout out 'Aberdeen' when the team names were being decided. David McLachlan was a Hibs supporter and he got in there first.

Continuing with the misconception that we were a nautical organisation, at the end of the night, we had to stand to attention in our teams and sing our anthem which was the chorus of the hymn, *We have an anchor*:

We have an anchor that keeps the soul,
Steadfast and sure while the billows roll,
Fastened to the Rock which cannot move,
Founded firm and deep in the Saviour's love.

Chapter Five – Boats and the Sea

Obviously, living by the sea, boats of all shapes and descriptions were a big part of our lives.

Already I've talked about the puffers bringing malt to the Distillery. It was quite fortunate for them if they got a return cargo to Glasgow, so when there were enough casks of matured whisky to fill a puffer, the hold would have been filled and I'm sure the cargo was appreciated because empty puffers sat very high in the water and danced like corks in a heavy sea. There was a very famous saying by deckhands on the puffers when they acted as banksmen. The winch operator stood beside the mast as that's where the control lever was. If, for example, the men in the hold were working out of the operator's line of vision, a member of the crew acted as his eyes and ears from outside the hold. When the malt bags, or empty casks, were securely fastened onto the hooks, ready for winching out of the hold, the instruction was to gently take the strain, then when everything was clear of the men, the next call was, **'Give her Six.'** I presume the winch was graded from one (slowest) to six (full speed) on the operating panel. We used to often come out with that saying when playing on our bikes and we were heading somewhere at full speed.

Other common cargoes into Bruichladdich pier were empty casks, bulk coal and bulk lime for farms.

Most puffer loads provided opportunities for us as kids to get into a lorry. Bulk coal had an even shorter journey than malt into the Distillery, probably 300 yards from the pier entrance to the coal yard (The Coalree

Full casks being loaded into the hold of a puffer.

Credit – The Dan McDonald Collection, held by The Ballast Trust.

as it was known). Bulk lime was distributed to local farms for spreading on fields at a later date. Usually the lime came in during school term time so little opportunity for us to spend the day in a lorry.

One task I often got on days when a puffer came in with distillery cargo, e.g., casks or malt, was to be sent round some houses in the village with a message. Puffers usually came in to Bruichladdich no more than one or two per week so it was all part-time casual labour that was used. I'd be sent to houses (hardly any would have phones) to tell the local men when they were needed the next day. Sometimes, after the boat had gone, I'd have to go round with their pay packet, always a small brown envelope with cash and no details whatsoever on the outside. Being paid in cash was always a very touchy and serious business. I was also paid in cash when I first started with J&B Scotland at Auchroisk Distillery in Banffshire. Pay packets, although containing a payslip inside, had basic details of gross pay and deductions on the front. When the manager handed the packet over, it was always handed with the front facing downwards so that nobody else got a glimpse. It was a correct and respectful way to do it, but the funny thing was, as soon as everyone got theirs, they would open it and then compare the contents with everyone else. Sometimes a distillery worker would be in a working position where he couldn't be reached by the manager, say at the top of high warehouse racking. I've had such an occasion when I was operating the cask stacker and I was handed someone's pay packet to pass on. Believe me, the Manager's (Dad) eyes and the recipient's eyes were trained on me, ensuring that not once did I get an opportunity to glance at the front of his envelope.

Other visiting ships were the coasters *Glenshiel* and *Glenshira*. Incidentally, there's an administration tale I read about the *Glenshiel*. She was actually officially registered in the Ship's Registry as *Glen Shiel* (two words) but instead of altering the apparent administration error on the paperwork, her owners chose to have ambiguous spacing of the lettering on her hull so that it wasn't obvious whether it was one word or two. The Glenlight company, owners of the *Glenshiel*, had a subsidiary company called Glen Line and there is a rumoured theory that they bought a vessel called the *Stentor* and renamed her *Glenshiel* also and it wasn't permitted to have two duplicate ships' names on the same registry. They were bigger than puffers but much less frequent visitors - more chance of them bringing in loads of fertiliser on behalf of Islay Farmers Ltd. One load however really sparked interest at the pier. In the mid to late 60s, the *Glenshiel* brought a new oil-fired boiler for Bruichladdich Distillery. This was a totally different proposition than normal cargoes. Instead of tying up at the end of the pier, she came right round the wooden pier and berthed at the concrete side of the pier at high tide, then beached herself at low tide. I'd never seen such a sight. She looked enormous, being so close to the shore. I'm sure it was a once in a lifetime sight for most of us in the village. Winching the boiler off was a major operation using an onboard crane. I remember Dad overseeing every single stage, standing in his brown dust coat, hands in pockets. Nothing happened without his say-so. Unfortunately, we were all in school when the boiler was transported to the Distillery but apparently it was pulled on a very low flat trailer. Again, being young, I never realised I was witnessing a huge change from coal-fired boilers to heavy-oil fired. Another knife in the back for our beloved puffers.

Dad overseeing boiler being unloaded from Glenshiel.

Credit – Family photo.

One Saturday afternoon in the early sixties, there was a huge gale. We were shopping in Bowmore when the gale reached its strongest point so Dad decided we should head for home. As we drove into Bruichladdich we could see activity on the road and shoreline in front of our house. I can recall looking along the shore and I've never seen so much foam created by the pounding waves. There were men trying to salvage empty casks which had blown out of the distillery yard, across the road and into the sea. It was surreal watching from the house window as the foam was lifted by the wind, engulfing the men who, bravely, managed to recover most of the casks . It wasn't till the gale had subsided that I noticed a large section in the middle of the wooden part of the pier had fallen victim to the weather and fallen into the sea. I was desperate to go out and watch everything that was going on but for once was firmly told to stay indoors.

One type of visiting boats which we loved seeing, but whose cargoes didn't spark any interest, because they never involved lorries, were the bulk heavy-oil tankers. Two vessels seemed to take it in turn to come,

Esso Brixham. Regular deliveries to Bruichladdich along with her sister ship Esso Poole.

Credit – Malcolm Cranfield

the *Esso Poole* and the *Esso Brixham*. I've just had a brain freeze, as I was just about to write that we took so little interest in the tankers that we didn't even bother to find out which company they belonged to. Until, of course, I noticed that they have the name 'Esso' in their titles. Oops!!

MacBrayne's cargo boats were a massive influence in the village. There was even something quite sentimental about the company name David MacBrayne Ltd on paperwork, lorries and signage, instead of the modern CalMac branding. The *Loch Ard* and very occasionally the *Loch Broom* kept the village and the Rhinns stocked with groceries, farm supplies and general cargo. I never appreciated at the time that the *Loch Ard* was built in 1955, the year I was born, so she was a relatively new boat and always looked immaculate. (One sad task while looking up dates that boats operated, and something I really haven't considered over the years, is the unfortunate fate of those old favourites who served us so well. The *Loch Ard* was scrapped in Bilbao in Northern Spain in 1985, while the *Loch Broom* tragically sank near Andros in Greece in 1974, both only thirty years old.) All cargo was winched from the boat in nets or cages and placed on flat bed trolleys and driven to the shed at the top of the pier. Then every single item was manhandled into the shed and on holidays, as well as the number of local men involved, us kids joined in. Looking at it now it was the most laborious time-consuming task ever. Taking groceries for example, the stock for six or seven shops was completely jumbled on the trolley. Each box of tinned goods, boxes of cereal packets, and packs of general groceries had to be picked up, one person read the label and shouted out the shop name, and a constant stream of men carried them to the part of the shed allocated to that shop. The shop goods were then distributed by MacBrayne's own lorry over the next few days and again each box had to be manhandled back out of the store and individually carried into the shops. It's pretty obvious why nowadays such goods are transported to shops by one man in a lorry with cages or pallets, but in those days, we didn't know any different and it was character-building for us kids to be involved with all the men.

Cargo ship M.V. Loch Ard.

Credit – Bill Tomlinson Collection.

Not all goods coming in by cargo boat were so small and easily handled. Occasionally there would be heavier bags of fertiliser or animal feeds, handled in exactly the same way into the shed before distribution. These were much heavier so the men had to handle them. I remember calves quite often going away. For easier handling, and their own safety, they were put in hessian bags with just their heads sticking out. Farmers would drive down the pier just minutes before the boat sailed, to cause minimal stress to the animals. They, and the live lobsters, were loaded and literally within minutes the boat cast off and headed down the loch.

Another much heavier type of goods was 45-gallon drums of

petrol for the pumps at Mackenzie's shop in Port Charlotte. These were steel drums with two heavy steel rings around the centre. Obviously a dangerous type of content, but manhandled in every stage of delivery. Once taken off the boat, they were rolled into the shed. On delivery day, they had to be rolled up a ramp onto the lorry, then at the petrol pumps, they were slowly rolled off the side of the lorry onto a pile of old car tyres and rolled into place. I went with the lorry quite often but after what I thought was 'helping' on one occasion, I had to watch from a safe distance in future deliveries. The storage tank for the petrol was directly below the pumps outside the shop window. The men opened a manhole cover on the ground and there was a hatch cover directly below. The idea, once the drum was off the lorry, was to position it close to the manhole, unscrew the cap off the barrel, then roll it forwards half a rotation and with the cap hole of the barrel now downwards, the petrol decanted into the storage tank below. So simple, what could go wrong? Well, the simple answer to that is that if you want it to go wrong, let a ten-year-old boy do it. Or more precisely, a ten-year-old boy did it without asking, trying to be helpful, while the men were chatting. I positioned a drum, unscrewed the cap, rolled it forward, but when the hole was at the bottom, it was nowhere near the tank so petrol was decanting onto the concrete and across the road. Instead of rolling the drum backwards, I just shouted, 'Look what's happened!' as though it was the drum's fault. I've never seen the men move so quickly to get the drum upright and I was called a few choice names. I think 'Interfering boy' was one of the least rude names I'm allowed to print.

Of course, back to the unloading of the boat at the storage shed, it wasn't all work, and you can't have a bunch of children helping all day without some sort of mischief, and we were no exception.

I think the men needed eyes in the back of their heads sometimes.

We'd jump on and off the trolleys as they were driven up and down the pier. They had solid tyres and bounced about, when empty, on the rough concrete surface, so it was great fun trying to stand up. Our favourite prank in the storage shed was to find a split box (if there wasn't a split box, we'd 'accidentally' find one) of packets of jelly, and we'd hide down behind the stack of boxes and tuck in.

This leads me to a story regarding my naivety as an eight-year-old boy. One day in 1963, a shining new Silver Cross pram, wrapped in cardboard with the wheels protruding, came off the *Loch Ard*. One of the men approached me with it and I thought he was going to ask me to put it at the back of the shed. But no, he said to me, 'Young Logie, take this to your mother.' I thought I'd misheard so I questioned what he said and he repeated, 'Wheel this thing to your mother, it's got her name on it.' We never disobeyed anything the men told us to do so off I toddled, wearing dungarees and wellies, pushing a pram through the village. I can picture it now, I was just passing the Abbotsford Hotel when I met one of the ladies from the village, heading for MacLeod's shop for her messages. We exchanged pleasantries and then she said, 'Where would you be going with that?' I just replied, 'To my Mum.'

I think you know what's coming next. 'Is she having a baby?'

'I don't know,' was my reply. Yes, as it happens, Mum was going to have a baby, my second sister Norma. But I obviously didn't see the signs, big belly, knitting baby cardigans, having a pram delivered, but at that particular moment, my priority as an eight-year-old boy, was to dump the pram at the house and get back to the important work of unloading the boat. Worrying about a new addition to the family was obviously a minor detail to a wee boy. In fact, come to think of it, I can remember exactly who Tish and I stayed with when Mum had to go to hospital in Glasgow, and I'm not sure if I even knew then that I was about to become a big brother.

A smaller boat, but big by skiff standards, spent more of the year in a shed at the pier than in the water but was very significant. I only ever remember seeing it anchored halfway between the pier and the Distillery and never saw it move but during several years she sat at anchor for one or two weeks in the summer. She was a magnificent blue colour (very apt considering its Conservative Party connection), was named *Our Ted*, and belonged to ex-Tory politician, leader of the Conservative Party and Prime Minister, Ted Heath. I believe he periodically holidayed at Islay House but I never set eyes on the man.

Archie Fletcher's white skiff was always moored at the steps on the concrete part of the pier. The only lobster fishermen in the village, John and Archie Fletcher headed out far down Lochindaal in the mornings to empty their lobster creels. This was considered to be too dangerous for youngsters to accompany them, and to be fair there probably wasn't enough room on the boat for anyone else, but it was their trips to sea in the evenings which interested me. The lobster pots were checked every morning, Monday to Saturday, and five evenings a week, at exactly 6.30 pm Archie would head out again to catch mackerel for bait. I remember sitting on our front doorstep waiting anxiously for Archie to come along the road and I never used to have to ask if I could go with him, he just beckoned me to follow. It was probably quite obvious to him that I was wanting to go out with him, because by the time my Mum had dressed me up in layers of jumpers and trousers, wellies, a hat and big coat, I resembled the Michelin Man rather than a keen amateur fisherman. Once on the boat, we'd usually head down the middle of the loch and see where the gannets were diving and that was the sure sign of a shoal of mackerel. I never tired of throwing a multi-hooked darrow line over the side and feeling the incredible tug of hooked mackerel. They were gorgeous as I pulled in the line with up to six silver fish, pulling in different directions, glistening in the water in the fading sunlight. A good catch for the evening with the two of us fishing would be just over one hundred fish. As we travelled between the fishing grounds and the pier, we'd often cast out a spinner hook in the hope of catching a cod, especially between Port Charlotte and Wester Ellister, on the Western side of the loch, and if we did, I got to take one home. On a school holiday, I'd sometimes venture to Archie's shed at the top of the pier in a morning, and he'd be preserving the previous night's mackerel catch by placing them, heavily salted, in wooden barrels.

MacBraynes and Western Ferries were the lifeline to the island. I have happy memories especially of going on the *Lochiel* on holiday. It was an adventure in itself getting to Port Askaig and Port Ellen, so going to the mainland by boat was a dream. The piers used to be absolutely buzzing with people, vehicles, animals, cargo etc. West Loch Tarbert pier was just amazing. Such a tight road and a tiny pier, but every square inch was used for cars, buses, cargo and pedestrians. It was best to get on the boat early, then get a bird's eye view from the upper deck of the loading. Cars (I think she only carried about eight) were loaded by driving onto two nets, one for each axle, and then lifted by derrick into the hold. Once ours was on, Dad would join us and he and I would watch everything and every person coming on board. It's not been unknown to share the passenger deck with a flock of sheep if they were going to the mainland.

The *Lochiel* was flat bottomed, specifically built to accommodate the shallow waters at West Loch Tarbert, our destination on the mainland. This made her very unstable and bouncy with the least bit of wind and waves, so many a time I felt a bit queasy, but as I have mentioned periodically, I'm a bit of a foodie, so when Mum brought out a picnic on the open deck, she had my full attention. Grudgingly, we used to throw crusts of bread to the seagulls who followed us all the way. I say grudgingly, it was my food, but it was also amazing watching them catch every morsel in flight before anything hit the water. Often, you'd see a crew member tip a bucket of food waste over the side and there was an almighty squawking frenzy as the gulls fought for the food before it sank.

There always seemed to be plenty to do, exploring the boat, getting to go and see the engine room, watching when the boat stopped and a little skiff would come out from the islands and meet us to drop off a passenger, and sometimes calling at Gigha pier. I remember there used to be a Border Collie dog on the pier and it loved chasing the ropes when thrown by the crew.

Lochiel at West Loch Tarbert pier.

Credit – Rod Lightbody.

Car being hoisted onboard Lochiel.

Credit – Rod Lightbody.

A couple of times Dad took me down a couple of decks to the bar on the *Lochiel*. That really was a man's world, not for a wee boy. I can only think that he would have taken me during rougher seas as I couldn't be trusted to behave on my own so he'd want to keep an eye on me. As if the *Lochiel* rolling from side to side wasn't enough, the smell of beer, the air full of cigarette smoke and seeing the waves splashing on the portholes made me a bit queasy. As if the constant rolling from side to side of the boat wasn't enough to make a young boy wonder if we'd ever get there safely (the crossing was about three and a half hours then), Dad decided to show me one day where the *Lochiel* once sank, in 1960, just short of West Loch Tarbert. That was just what I didn't want to know so I always breathed easy after we passed that spot. I mentioned earlier about sheep sometimes sharing part of the passenger deck space and that's exactly what happened the day she hit the rock. Unfortunately the sheep had to be released and chance finding their own way ashore.

One lovely memory of the *Lochiel* when I didn't have to board her was at the start of the traditional Glasgow Fair holiday fortnight. It was worth going to Port Ellen just to watch as she came in, absolutely jam-packed with holidaymakers and a piper would play on board as she approached the pier.

I've probably even less stories about Western Ferries. Their boats, *Sound of Islay* and *Sound of Jura* were resplendent in their red and white livery, and many times we'd go to the pier at Port Askaig just to watch how easy travel had become with roll-on/roll-off ferries.

Travelling on the new ferries was a novelty, especially driving on and off, or should I say reversing on and driving off. There were some hilarious attempts at reversing. Some of the crew would get frustrated at old lady drivers and they'd stick their arm in the open car window and steer for them. I have to say CalMac are very methodical in their loading now, but in the early Western Ferries days, you'd have two marshals shouting and gesticulating two different directions to one driver and seeing tempers getting raised was great entertainment. Seating areas were much more restricted than present-day ferries so it was a case of finding a seat and then keeping it because there wasn't a lot else to do.

One amazing change to our lives was getting Sunday newspapers on, wait for it, a Sunday. A car used to go round the island selling door to door, it got to Bruichladdich about 5 pm, and although we previously only ever bought one newspaper, the Sunday Post (on a Monday), all of a sudden, we had this novelty and Dad would send me out to the car to buy FIVE papers:

Sunday Post
Sunday Mail

The People

News of the World

Sunday Express.

Incidentally, I won the Sunday Post Quiz Cup in 1987 with a team of four from the engineering team with J&B Scotland in Banffshire. The quiz was always a popular go-to page in the paper. As a child, I never understood the attraction of having all these papers with the same news on the front page. As a twelve-year-old, my priority was the football pages with pictures of my beloved Aberdeen FC for my scrapbook.

Another boat I have a strong connection with and fondness for was the ex-passenger ship S.S. *Uganda*. I was once fortunate enough to go on her for a school cruise from Greenock to The Azores, Madeira, Lisbon and Vigo in Western Spain, finishing in Leith fourteen days later. The *Uganda* been converted to a cruise ship in 1967 with 920 dormitory berths and to us, was luxurious. I remember reading about ships' Quartermasters and I'm sure somebody wound me up before the cruise about how strict they were. Basically, they were nautical versions of Sergeant Majors. Well, we had a real loud character onboard and I'm still haunted by his early morning chorus. 'FEET ON THE DECK' he'd bellow as he opened the dormitory door and believe me, we leapt out of our bunks. You could hear his bellowing voice echo all the way down the corridor as he woke each room in turn.

There were lots of small school groups from various islands. I remember we got on particularly well with the Tiree school group. The ship's Captain also looked favourably on us and through our teacher Miss Bell, arranged that on a forthcoming cruise, he would pass through the Sound of Islay on a specific date and we could wave to him. Sure enough, the pier at Port Askaig was full on the night in question and although a couple of hours late, this majestic white liner seemed to fill the Sound as she steamed past us. By now it was about 9 pm and seeing her lit up was breathtaking. The sound of the ship's horn and all the parents blasting their car horns was deafening but it was a lovely gesture by the Captain and an evening to remember.

However, this wasn't to be my only encounter with the *Uganda*. She was adapted to become a vital hospital ship during the Falklands war in 1982. She had to cut short an educational trip in Naples, disembark her passengers, then head for a three-day refit in Gibraltar (including the fitting of a helicopter landing pad) before heading straight to the Falkland Islands. I served in the RAF from 1974 to 1986 and in May 1984 was chosen to serve a six-month tour in Port Stanley. We flew from RAF Brize Norton in Oxfordshire to Wideawake Airport on Ascension Island in the South Atlantic. Transfer to our waiting ship was by shaky old RAF Wessex helicopter and as we flew over South West Bay, I spotted my old friend S.S. *Uganda* waiting for us. She was now sadly a very tired, very dirty old ship. She'd been completely stripped of all cruise ship luxuries and was literally a floating dormitory.

S. S. Uganda.

Credit – Stig Baumeyer

One of the highlights during the eight-day journey through the South Atlantic was watching albatrosses with their enormous wingspans gliding inches over the waves, while the downside for a couple of days was in rough seas where you'd hear the propellers rumble as they came out of the water as the ship pitched in huge waves. Still, I enjoyed my eight day 'cruise' to the Falklands, accompanied by fellow RAF colleagues and hundreds of Scots Guards. I'm also glad I wasn't transferred to the Falklands aboard the other ship being used, H.M.S. Keren. She was a more flat bottomed ship and on reaching Port Stanley, sometimes she had to anchor for days at a time because the strong winds (the Falklands are notoriously windy) would have blown her onto the rocks at the narrow harbour entrance. Using the H.M.S. Keren was controversial because she was actually a cross channel ferry, the M.V. St Edmund, but she was acquired by the government during the Seaman's strike in 1983. As the crew refused to sail, she was commissioned as H.M.S Keren and a non-union and military crew were assembled.

Another sea-related tale was when I used to collect whelks on the seashore. After speaking to Archie Fletcher about where he sent his lobsters each week, he said they were boxed, put on the *Loch Ard* on her weekly visit, and they were transported to Billingsgate fish market in London. He said he'd contact his buyer and that if I decided to collect whelks, they could piggyback onto his delivery. Whelk collecting is back-breaking work and tide dependent, so if low tide is 5 am, then that's when you go out. During the school holidays, early starts were beautiful, watching the sunrise down on the shore. I collected about three hundredweight (150 kilos in today's money) per week. The whelks had to be kept fresh and alive so I kept them in hessian sacks in the sea beside the wee slipway at Bruichladdich pier. The night before the *Loch Ard* came, Dad would come and sew the bags shut and we'd fix a label for the Billingsgate wholesaler. MacBrayne's men carried the bags up to the pier for me and hey presto, next thing I knew was postal orders arriving in the mail a week later. I immediately cashed them in at the village Post Office to buy Premium Bonds which I still have to this day. Nothing ever went missing in transit and there were very few whelks discarded when sieved and graded for size in London. Of course, everything was done properly and I felt very grown-up going to MacBrayne's pier office once a week to pay my transport costs - 7/6d per bag.

Dad helping me sew up bags of whelks ready for transport to Billingsgate Market.

Credit – Family photo.

There's a postscript to this story. In 2008, when I was a Distillery Manager like my Dad, I was invited to a black-tie Dinner and Awards Ceremony at Old Billingsgate Market. The market was converted into an events venue in 1982 when it moved to new premises. At the dinner table, I sat next to a whisky journalist, and he was absolutely fascinated by my connection with Billingsgate Market, 40 years previously. He had planned to do an article on my whelk collecting and why Billingsgate was important in my life but we lost touch. And no, before anyone asks, I wasn't at the awards ceremony to receive an accolade, just a dinner guest.

Surprisingly, for a village right on the seashore, we had very little interest in swimming or being in the water. Going out on a boat, now that's a different story. The bits of beach within the village boundaries weren't spectacular, but still, none of us had any great desire to jump in. It was different during the summer holidays, especially when a few of the mums decided to take us to Portbahn, opposite Coultorsay farm. Sited at the foot of the rocks, below the war memorial, it always looked so special with the clear waves lapping the golden sand. Portbahn was actually two beaches although most people just bothered with the main larger beach on the North side. When lots of families went it was brilliant, sharing picnics and just a general buzz about the place. Families doing all this together was pretty rare in the village, and even the half-mile walk to the beach together was fun. It was also one of the rare times that several of the dads in the village interacted with the youngsters. I didn't even know Dad could swim till I was about ten, but obviously his Navy days were put to good use.

I still can't swim properly; a width of the local swimming pool is my limit. My own fault entirely, I've had ample opportunities since childhood, but it's quite embarrassing to admit, especially when people learn I was raised on an island.

I have a memory of a boat coming in by Bruichladdich pier with salvage. There was a time when some sunken ships off the west coast of Islay were being salvaged and one evening a few of us were playing around the pier area and we saw a boat in the distance so naturally we went to the end of the pier to investigate. It was a fishing boat which had never come in before so the closer it got, the more intrigued we were.

As it got really close, we could see it wasn't carrying any fishing gear, no nets or fish boxes, but there were ropes, gas cylinders and winches on the deck. Each of us stood beside a bollard on the pier as we enjoyed catching ropes and securing vessels but strangely, she stayed about 20 yards from the pier and appeared to be going past us. As it happened, she was going round the pier to beach her haul. We were so busy concentrating on the vessel that we almost missed what she was towing. She'd come from one of the wrecks and she was actually a diving support boat. If ever in my life I wanted to have a camera, it was then. A few feet under the surface, behind the boat, was the most majestic, glistening huge bronze propeller blade. It was stunning to see and seemed to glide effortlessly behind the tow rope. Obviously, it was too heavy to winch aboard so they were going to beach it and pull it ashore. What an unexpected and beautiful sight and such a change from the usual boats.

September 8th 1968 was a day that most of us on Islay wouldn't recall the exact date, but would remember the misty Sunday morning as the day the *Agios Minas* ran around north of Frenchman's Rocks, about two miles from Portnahaven. Again, as I mentioned in Chapter Three, coincidentally the *Agios Minas* was bound for Sharpness in the Bristol Channel, close to where I live now. She was a Liberian registered cargo vessel carrying timber, stacked high on her decks, and she inexplicably steered into the rocks and stuck fast. I remember by the time we heard about it and drove up there, every verge, gateway and every bit of field that was dry enough became a car park. Not having experienced very large boats visiting the island, nothing could really prepare me for the sad sight of this huge vessel, her decks laden with wood, 15ft high, as we came walking over the brow of the hill. So many people were on the shore watching helplessly and there was an eerie silence as she creaked with each wave wedging her into the rocks. Eventually the timber on deck broke free and equally saddening, and a danger to other boats, was the sight of a 'slick' of timber floating out to sea. Luckily there were no casualties and Islay lifeboat safely took the crew ashore, with the Coastguards and a tug, the Clyde-based *Cruiser*, in attendance.

Agios Minas.

Credit – Reproduced with kind permission of Scottishshipwrecks.com

Agios Minas.

Credit – Reproduced with kind permission of Scottishshipwrecks.com

Agios Minas.

Credit – Alan Turner-Smith, Yeovil.

Agios Minas.

Credit – Alan Turner-Smith, Yeovil.

We visited the wreck site several times, once spending a good part of a day watching a helicopter salvaging wood and scrap from the ship as she'd been declared a wreck. Stories circulated the island for months about people finding good timber on various parts of Islay's shoreline and stashing it safely in case Her Majesty's Customs took an interest. A bit of a modern-day *Whisky Galore*.

Coincidentally, I stumbled upon Agios Minas (Saint Minas, in English) Cathedral in Heraklion, the capital of Crete, while on holiday there in 2022.

In May 1964, I witnessed (from a distance) part of a huge operation to transport a new boiler to Bowmore Distillery. I wish I'd been taken to see the whole unloading effort, but from Bruichladdich we could see the landing craft anchored off the distillery. It transpired that this boat had sailed from Rhu Naval Base with the new boiler from Renfrew. It was quite eerie yet exciting as such an unusual boat was across the water from our house and she sat motionless as the sea glistened as the rising sun tried to break through the mist. There are several YouTube videos available, recording the whole journey.

Chapter Six – Other Transport

The daily plane service to Glasgow was and is a vital service. Apart from flying to Islay when we moved there, I think I flew once more using the BEA service while going on holiday, probably around 1967.

However, I was unfortunate enough to have appendicitis in 1968 and so Dr Tait summoned the ambulance plane from Glasgow. Everything was a bit rushed and the ambulance was at the house within the hour. Dad quickly made the decision to travel with me so he had to organise who would look after his beloved Distillery. Off we set to the airport at Glenegadale and on a couple of occasions I caused a bit of panic with the pain I was in and the ambulance had to stop opposite Island Farm as I was nauseous. I suppose the risk of an appendix bursting on a remote island is pretty dangerous so everyone kept making sure I was ok and stayed awake.

Ambulance plane.

Credit – Rod Lightbody.

My next memory is of the inside of the ambulance plane, my stretcher on the port side and Dad with the nurse on the starboard. I tried all sorts of positions to stop the stinging pains and eventually found that sitting up on the stretcher was best. My geography was quite good and as we followed the River Clyde towards Glasgow, I started pointing out things and places I recognised. So much so that I started to enjoy myself. There was a puffer, MacBrayne's ferries, tankers, fishing boats, high rise flats. I was on a roll and kept making sure that Dad could see everything that interested me. I had no appreciation of the sacrifice he'd made by packing a bag in an hour and potentially leaving the Distillery for a few days.

On one occasion, with about ten minutes of the flight to go, the nurse had to go forward to the cockpit to speak to the ambulance plane Captain, just as I excitedly told Dad about something else I'd seen. I think he saw red mist as this terribly sick boy from an hour ago had suddenly become the most hyperactive person on the plane. In the absence of the nurse, he leaned across the stretcher, looked me square in the eye and said, 'You bloody well better be ill, boy.'

Anyway Dad, I didn't let you down, my appendix came out that afternoon in the Western Infirmary and I wasn't bluffing.

I think Dad got his wee bit of revenge once I was in the hospital ward, prior to diagnosis being confirmed. I just remember a sea of white coats and this eccentric-looking surgeon (wearing a bow tie was eccentric to me) came to my bedside. The first question he asked was, 'Have your bowels moved today?' Well, he may as well have been talking in Chinese. How the hell did he expect this ill, nervous, island boy to know what a bowel was and whether it had moved anywhere. Dad was on the other side of the bed and just shook his head and the surgeon made some notes. (My little imagination was now in overdrive. If this bowel thing has moved - where is it now?)

Next came the physical test to prove appendicitis. The surgeon pressed his straight fingers against my stomach and pushed hard before releasing quickly. Wow, the pain. But he said, 'That's good,' and repeated it another two or three times. The old guy is probably six feet under now, but I can assure him it was anything but 'good' when you're on the receiving end. Then, once I'd got my breath back, and decided that surely life couldn't get any more cruel today, old bow tie man asked Dad, not me, if his six accompanying students could have a go. Dad of course said, 'Yes, by all means.' God, there are some cruel people in this world. If I didn't feel sore when I came in to hospital, I damn well did now. My poor wee stomach was pushed in and recoiled so many times and each time I winced in pain, the students were congratulated on finding the spot and confirming what we already knew.

Another mode of transport, that unfortunately only broke down once, was Caskie's bus to Bowmore School. On the one occasion it broke down, someone (I bet it was my Mum), foolishly phoned the Distillery. Quick as a flash, before we could all disperse to enjoy a day off, the Distillery's brand spanking new Land Rover appeared with strict instructions to take us to school. This was unfair, what about all the lucky people from Portnahaven and Port Charlotte who got a day off. Why didn't the Ballygrant or Port Ellen bus come and pick them up. Nobody forced them into private transport. Not a happy bunch of kids that day.

The 'bus stop' in Bruichladdich was Olive McLachlan's front porch at the croft house. A lovely warm little refuge, although if everyone squeezed in on a rainy day, it was extremely packed. I had another reason to like the porch. Although you could see it from our house, you couldn't see through the net curtains. Now Mum and Dad were very strict about school uniform, but if I was quick enough in the mornings, I could get into the porch before everyone else and change my clothes. So I'd sneak out of the house, big thick jumper on, and after one minute in the porch, I removed it to reveal my Bay City Rollers tartan shirt. I nearly got caught out a few times by forgetting to change back to the original dull jumper before I got home.

I suppose this counts as transport, although I've no idea what kind. All I remember is that there was a delivery to the Post Office at 5pm on a Saturday evening. There was a bit of competition amongst some of the boys in the village to get to the Post Office first and take a bundle of newspapers to MacLeod's shop. I was successful on a good few occasions, and my reward was always a Toffee Crisp bar. Yay, more food.

On one other Saturday evening, I wasn't at the Post Office doing my newspaper run, but Dad received a phone call from a very agitated Greta. In fact, it was a delirious Greta. She'd received a mail bag as usual. From the virtually screaming voice on the phone, we reckoned something was up. She'd stuck her hand in the mailbag to pick out the first handful of letters, only to grab two pheasants round the neck. I'm sure her heart must have stopped momentarily. Some company from the mainland had sent Dad two pheasants, no wrapping, just a label tied round their necks. 'Get your boy to come over straight away' was her instruction, but I bet that from then on, she'd have been a lot more cautious putting her hand blindly into mail sacks.

Anyone on Islay would offer a lift in those days. A great unofficial taxi, if you weren't in a hurry was the milk lorry. The lorry would go round all the dairy farms collecting milk churns to take to the Creamery in Port Charlotte. Islay cheese was popular in the UK and across Europe, famously being banned in Italy for its alleged aphrodisiac qualities. A lot of the farms would take their churns to the roadside where the lorry would pick them up and leave empties for the next day. If I was going up to Kilchiaran to play with Neil McLellan, I'd wait at the milk stand beside the croft next door and jump in the lorry when it arrived. We'd have a few more stops along the way and then go into the Creamery to offload. Then we'd be off again to pick up the rest of the day's churns from the Portnahaven side and get dropped off at Kilchiaran eventually.

The following may sound a strange tale but it didn't really fit in any other chapter. So, the fact is that on the mainland, when driving to West Loch Tarbert, we often saw travelling people in their tents by the roadside between Lochgilphead and Tarbert. I'm loathed to be disrespectful and call them by what we used to say, but the dictionary backs me up by referring to the dated Scottish slang name of 'Tinkers'. You knew they were headed for Islay when larger groups of tents gathered by the roadside near the ferry. Often, they worked on farms, especially thinning neeps.

One day in the mid 60s, Mum was on her own in our house and a travelling lady came to the front door. Mum was asked if she wanted to buy any tea towels, clothes pegs, cloths, dusters etc. and she politely declined. However, the lady persevered and eventually Mum told her quite emphatically that the answer was 'No'. This led the lady to start cursing and she left, but not before telling Mum that she'd put a curse on her and told her what year she was going to die. Now if you think Mum was harsh, let me tell you that Dad would never ever, in a million years, buy anything like this, door to door. So imagine Mum's surprise when Dad came home for his tea at half past five as usual, with a handful of tea towels. Dad just said, 'I got these for you, they'll be handy,' and remained totally tight-lipped when Mum enquired about why and where he'd bought them.

It became obvious to her that the lady had gone next door to the Distillery Office and must have scared the living daylights out of Dad because normally, he'd have argued all day rather than buy such items.

Mum never knew if he'd been told of the 'curse' put on her, or if he'd received news of his own fate. For information, Mum would happily tell the story but would never confide in us what the year of her predicted death was. Suffice to say that by 2010, she told us that the year had passed without incident.

Chapter Seven – Working at Bruichladdich Distillery

Dad worked at Bruichladdich Distillery for twelve years, so as a family we're all proud of my nephew Calum who is currently employed there. Officially, Calum is third generation at Bruichladdich Distillery because I was on the books in the summer of 1970 as a fifteen-year-old. I was employed virtually just doing one job, namely stencilling the ends of empty casks. Nowadays, many distilleries staple a single barcode to one end of each cask and the information on it far outweighs what used to be written on the end staves. However, in the past both ends were stencilled and firstly, writing Bruichladdich Distillery Proprietors Limited around the circumference was a task in itself. Then once the cask number and the year of filling was added, all the casks for the filling, about eighty, were turned over and stencilled on the other end. I hold my hands up and admit that a couple of times, the writing was the right way up on one end and upside down on the other. That was a lesson you learned very quickly. At that time, the empty cask store was above where the shop is now. The smell of oak, the dingy darkness from so few windows, was just so atmospheric and timeless.

It was my first official paid job, and having tea breaks with my first Thermos flask and a couple of rolls Mum made for me, was like a picnic every day. It felt so grown up, being with all the men in the new canteen, the air full of cigarette smoke, but I didn't mind. Some of the older men seemed to take an eternity to clean out, refuel and light their pipes. They must only have got a few puffs before going back to work. Each had his own tiny thin knife to scrape the old tobacco from the bowl of the pipe and each had his own meticulous method of tapping the pipe, paring tobacco from a solid block and tightly packing down before the routine of relighting.

Although nothing to do with me working at the Distillery, this next tale annoyed the hell out of Dad at the time, and he relayed the story for years afterwards to anyone who would listen. Mum and Dad's bedroom was at the front of the house. One night, about 2 or 3 am, Dad was asleep but became agitated when he thought he heard the slightest tapping noise. He tossed and turned for a while and continued to hear this quiet tap tap tap. Was he imagining it, or was something flapping in the wind outside. It wasn't a mouse, it was too dark outside to be a bird, but sure enough, there it was again, tap tap tap. He thought, 'enough's enough' so he got out of bed and walking past the curtains, there was this bloody annoying little tapping again. He flung the curtain open, and there was the stillman grinning and about to tap again. Dad opened the window and said, 'What on earth's going on?' (I'm sure that's a cleaned-up version).

'Mr Logie, the new boiler's broken down and I can't start it.'

'Why the hell didn't you bang on the window instead of damn well tapping?' Dad said.

'Ah well Mr Logie, I didn't want to wake Mrs Logie.'

Dad never relayed how that story finished but I'm sure the air was blue for a while. And of course, Mum was now wide awake with all the commotion going on, so an unsuccessful attempt at trying not to wake her.

Chapter Eight – Shopping

There were two shops in Bruichladdich, MacLeod's at the top of the pier road, and the Co-op (now Bruichladdich Mini Market, or Debbie's) between the croft and the doctor's. To a child, I suppose the Co-op appeared like a modern-day supermarket - it felt huge - but I was normally only sent there for essentials as it was slightly closer to our house. I always remember at the end of your purchase, you had to recite your Co-op dividend number. Ours was 1368 - funny how some minor details stick in your head 60 years later.

I'm afraid I got a humiliating telling-off round the back of the Co-op one day, in front of my friends, and then frog-marched home. It was the day MacBrayne's lorry delivered the boxes of groceries from the *Loch Ard's* previous visit. I helped load the lorry at the pier with Allistair and a couple of MacBrayne's men. To get to the Co-op, we sat in the trailer on top of a couple of boxes. Of course, even for a two-minute drive we had to mess about and fight, and stupidly, I allowed myself to fall backwards off the box directly outside our house. And naturally my policewoman of a mother was looking directly at me from the living room window. How she did it I don't know, but the lorry had only reversed up to the back door of the Co-op, and she was standing there. No amount of excuses about the lorry braking (which was a lie), Allistair pushed me (also a lie), were listened to. It was straight home, confined to the house and not allowed out in the evening, even to go mackerel fishing with Archie Fletcher.

MacLeod's shop was legendary. Mr and Mrs MacLeod were both always there, day and night. The odd couple of Bruichladdich, he was fairly tall, calm and quiet spoken, she was short, excitable and waddled like a duck. The arguments they used to have were hilarious; poor woman couldn't do anything right in his eyes, and he used to lose his temper so quickly. Absolutely nothing like a modern-day shop, it was just a room in their house with shelving, some glass cabinets and a table at first, and then they extended and opened a second bigger room with a huge table in the middle. So everything really centred around the first room, and if you asked for anything that was displayed in the other room, Alec would go and get it for you. Now, as kids, we quickly latched onto the fact that if you asked for something from room two, he'd get it for you, then we'd immediately ask for something else from the next room, and he'd roll his eyes and mutter something about, 'Make your mind up'. There was always the chance he'd bump into his wife in the doorway too, causing him further stress. Alec was meticulously calm and deliberate in everything he did (apart from when we wound him up), and I have to give him his due, I've never seen anyone pack groceries into a cardboard box so neatly. Before the days of carrier bags, you'd always be offered a box.

I always had a routine when I came home from Gortan School. I'd get changed, then had to go to MacLeod's for the Daily Record. There was always a biscuit tin on the table in the kitchen of the house, so I'd shout through to Mum in the living room, 'Can I take a biscuit?' She always said I could, but I couldn't resist taking at least four. I wonder if she ever counted them.

One Saturday evening, Dad caused a bit of consternation in MacLeod's shop. I was playing in the front garden, and Dad asked if I wanted to go to the shop with him. That was his only ever venture to the shop, occasional Saturday evenings, and it only meant one thing - bars of chocolate for

Allistair and myself with a young Norma and Tibby the pet lamb.

Credit – Family photo.

the family before we sat down to watch the Black and White Minstrel Show. I thought to myself that there was no real need for me to go, I'd get my chocolate anyway. However, when I saw that Dad was taking our pet sheep Tibby for a walk on her lead, I thought, 'This could be fun.' Tibby was an orphan lamb we hand reared and kept on the front lawn and gradually we trained her to walk with a dog's lead. By now she was fully grown. Off we went to the shop, I went in first because I wasn't going to miss any of the action. In came Dad and Tibby and when Mrs MacLeod saw her, she screamed and waddled through to the back of the shop. The aisles were narrow, usually because there were boxes everywhere, so what's the worst thing you can do to a highly strung sheep? Yes, scream at her, and so Tibby decided she didn't want to be there any more. She reared up like a stallion, then knocked boxes with her bum, and we'd only got as far as the lobby. Dad asked me to take Tibby out, and he never repeated the scenario. I don't suppose he'd ever want the headline 'Distillery Manager With Rampaging Sheep Banned From Shop'.

Chapter Nine – Dad's Beasts

Dad loved the thought of being a small-time crofter and he kept a few animals on the fields owned by the Distillery. I think the most he would have had at any one time would be three bullocks, about twelve sheep and ten chickens. Some crofters worked at the Distillery, some helped out with emptying and loading puffers, and in general he got to know most neighbouring crofters and some local farmers through selling draff to them. Being a complete novice when we moved to Islay, he learned quickly and used every opportunity to learn from anyone who offered their experience. Both my sisters went on to marry farmers so Dad always had questions for them.

I loved helping with the sheep, especially when we had to hand-rear lambs. Most of his work on his 'croft' was done in the evenings and if there were any big jobs like clipping or dosing, local crofters would lend a hand. I loved being involved and I loved listening to all the men talking, they seemed to know so much.

Again, after showing such naivety with the pram story in Chapter Five, I wasn't much better when it came to the business side of crofting. As I said, Dad usually had three bullocks and he was usually quite upfront with me about selling them. Often, they were different ages and he'd take me to the field in an evening and tell me that one of them was being sold next day. It didn't dawn on me that there were no sales on the next day, just that some mysterious buyer was taking one of our animals. Next day after school I'd go and check the field and sure enough there were

A very young Graham feeding one of our orphan lambs.

Credit – Family photo.

now two beasts where there were three yesterday. It wasn't emotional, just reality because that's what happened in crofts all around us.

However, about two days later, Mum would announce that everyone was to stay in that evening because Dad had managed to purchase the meat from an entire bullock and we were all to be involved in helping put everything in bags for the freezer. This was exciting and sure enough Dad would appear home after being at Roy's slaughter house in Port Charlotte, and he had trays of mince, steaks, beef joints etc for us to pack. Generally, with the whole family together in the kitchen, the conversation was about school etc, and if ever I asked about the meat, I was fobbed off with the answer that Dad had got a considerably good price for our animal, and immediately bought all this meat with the money he'd made. I think I was actually quite proud of him. Goodness knows how many years later, it dawned on me that two days after we sold every animal, an entire carcass appeared in our kitchen. I'd been eating Daisy, Meg, Bess and all the other beautiful friends I'd named, for all these years, and never once did the coincidental timing cross my mind.

Dad used to winter the bullocks in an old shed behind Mr and Mrs MacKenzie's house. I remember him going away once on business and he trusted me to feed the beasts for about four nights. I had to take a couple of pails of draff with me that the distillery workers had put aside for me during the day, a good armful of hay each and three neeps between them, chopped into slices with a spade. I felt so grown up, going out in the dark to feed them, and of course I took my time because I could hardly be told off for being out so long when I was being so responsible. However, there were also some wrecks of old cars beside the shed, probably 1940s or 1950s models with lots of bits missing but importantly, they had a steering wheel, so after fulfilling my 'adult' duties feeding the livestock, I'd sit in the cars and the wee boy was back where he belonged, making screeching noises and turning the steering wheel from side to side as though I was Jackie Stewart.

Opposite the Coalree on the South end of the village, there was a circle of land completely surrounded by thick whin bushes. It was between MacLeod's shop and Mrs Gillespie's, where Gleaner's depot is now, and had a high stone wall along the roadside, so very secluded. Dad decided to put a henhouse there and a heap of chickens and a cockerel appeared overnight. Goodness knows where they came from, little boys weren't privy to that sort of detail, and neither were we interested. It was a great novelty accompanying Dad to feed the hens in the mornings, collect the eggs, and then lock them in at night. There was something really comforting in the evenings, just before dark, when we'd open the henhouse door and all the hens would be on the perches, huddled together. They seemed so content and safe.

Naturally not everything went so smoothly when I wasn't accompanied. One Saturday morning, Mum said Dad was busy, and was I able to feed the hens on my own. I said, 'Of course' but I was also thinking about how nothing could possibly go wrong with such an easy task. After getting my usual lecture about 'Mind the road now' (in one ear and out the other, I'd heard it so often), I took the can of food, walked down the road, and climbed over the stile to the henhouse. I opened the door as usual, loved listening to the appreciative noise of the hens as they ate the food I was slowly scattering, and just patted myself on the back for being so helpful and trustworthy. Next minute - pandemonium. The cockerel thought he'd show me who was boss. Wings flapping, he chased me, pecked my legs, flew up shoulder height, oh my God I'd never been attacked before. The more I ran, he ran too and I hadn't the sense to head straight for the stile to get out. In fact I headed for the bushes and couldn't get through. I swear not a single hen even lifted her head, nothing was more important than eating. I was in a total panic but eventually managed to find the stile and step over the wall.

I never collected the eggs, just ran home and reported that the crazy cockerel had attacked me. I could immediately tell no-one appreciated my life had been in danger and I was lucky to get out with both my eyes intact. Dad was home by this time, so he took me back there. That damn cockerel strutted about as though butter wouldn't melt in his mouth. Dad muttered something like, 'What have you been up to today then, my lad?' to him, like a devoted father speaking to a baby. We got the eggs and left, and I'm positive that Dad was wondering what all the fuss was about. It was probably assumed that since I was always doing something wrong, I'd been up to my tricks and upset the cockerel. In my defence, when I told Tish that I was going to mention the livestock in the book, and the novelty of keeping hens, all she said was 'Be sure to mention the bloody crazy cockerel.' So I wasn't the only one to be scared of it. I don't know if anyone's noticed that, unlike the bullocks, the cockerel didn't have a name. I called him plenty of names that morning, believe me.

One day, we came home from Gortan School, and something in the village seemed a wee bit different. We saw a small skiff halfway across Lochindaal but never really took much notice. Mum was in the front garden, looking out across the water, very unusual as she was always indoors when I got home, and a couple of the Distillery workers were down on the shore. I asked what was going on and Mum told me that Dad was one of the men in the boat, and he was chasing a bullock.

This took a bit of believing, sounds like the sort of fairy tale that a wee boy would conjure up. But no, that's exactly what was happening. Apparently, Dad had been moving his beasts through the village to a new pasture, and as always, two or three people helped to make sure they didn't stray off into gardens etc. One bullock got startled and instead of the usual mad dash to get into another field, or bolt up the wrong road, this one headed straight for the sea and just swam. I think it took all the men by surprise, and they would have been convinced it would turn around, but no, it kept going, heading apparently for Bowmore! Somebody got into a boat, made sure there were ropes handy and took Dad out to sea. By this time the escaped bullock was well out and even when they overtook him, he still didn't turn around. They managed to get a rope round his neck and drag him round to face Bruichladdich again and the slow swim home started. Unbelievably, they all made it back safely and the beast wasn't too difficult to walk to the field, he was absolutely knackered. I don't know what name we'd given him prior to that but he should certainly have been re-christened 'Lucky', he must have been swimming for over forty-five minutes.

Chapter Ten – Crofts

Crofts surrounded the village and were great fun to be around. Neil McLachlan's next door was the most accessible and I spent countless hours playing football in his stackyard (so called because that's where the hay and corn stacks were built. Harvest time was busy and the stackyard was full of men. Hay ricks were brought from the fields using a tractor and buckrake, corn sheaves were brought in on a trailer. Then stacks were built to store the feed through the winter). Myself, big Neilly, David McLachlan and James McEachern would play two-a-side using my big heavy lace-up leather football. When it was raining, the ball weighed a ton, but I felt unstoppable in my new Bobby Charlton boots. Hang on, he's a World Cup winner You'll read later why I'm haunted by that damn cup.

Every Sunday morning, I was made to clean my football boots and rub them with Dubbin wax for waterproofing. I loved the smell of Dubbin and I've never even seen a tin, let alone used it for the last fifty-five years, but I've just Googled it and it's still available to buy.

Thinning turnips was a day when everyone got involved. Knee pads were hessian sacks tied round our legs with baler twine. The secret was to do a drill each and if we all went the same speed, we could chat and joke together.

Spreading fertiliser was amazing when Neil did it by hand. The boys would stand in each corner of the field where there were several fertiliser bags stacked. Neil was a big man and he had a round metal tray, suspended by a rope round his neck. He'd fill it with fertiliser and walk up and down the field casting fertiliser with each hand, left then right, until he'd emptied the carrier. He then walked to the nearest boy to refill from the bags. I was always amazed by his strength. I'd pour fertiliser into the carrier until he winced in pain and he'd still ask for more.

Taking home peats was always a great day out. The Clydesdale horse was set up with the cart and we'd all pile onboard for the trip up the hill behind Conisby to the moss. After piling the cart high with peats, we'd have to walk back down the hill. The views over Lochindaal were spectacular and we still had the energy to run about through the heather.

Looking back, I now think it's comical when I read of kids, from all different walks of life, and different parts of the country, and they talk about pinching (scrumping) apples from neighbours' gardens, or maybe sneaking a strawberry or a pea pod when they weren't meant to. Not in Bruichladdich, that was far too small a haul for us. Our favourite 'snack' was to find a field of turnips ready to lift. Best if they were up the Conisby road, out of sight, and it also gave us time to gorge ourselves on the way home. None of us carried knives, so we'd get a decent-sized turnip, peel it by glancing blows on a fence post, then devour it on the way down the hill. Invariably, this was immediately before teatime but it was no problem eating a two-course meal straight away.

The Distillery dam is located up on the hill above Gartacharra. In the summertime we'd be up the Gartacharra road every evening when Dad had to go and regulate the amount of water coming down to the Distillery. The better the summer weather, the more the water flow had to be restricted. There was so much to see, sheep, nesting birds, the occasional adder if we were lucky. We had a pet poodle, Pippin (named after Norma's favourite comic), and he'd come with us every evening. I suppose we walked almost a mile from the house to the dam, but Pippin probably ran about seven miles in that time. We hardly saw him, just seeing where he ran as the heather parted where he was running. At age seven, Pippin, who was black, started turning grey and slowed down considerably. Dad was a wee bit worried and took him to the vet, who said that all the crazy running about had literally aged him before his time.

Harvest time was always an attraction. Baling hay and straw, then taking the bales home were adventures. Obviously getting lifts in the trailer was great fun, especially if we were sitting on top of bales. There was always a chance to drive tractors in the fields as the men were far stronger to throw the bales up onto the trailer. A great attraction was when Gartacharra got the threshing mill out, usually just behind Burnside and on a Saturday morning. The boys didn't really get much to do as it was heavy and dangerous work but all the men were brilliant with us and it felt like a community exercise. We did enjoy when most of a corn stack had been fed into the threshing mill, and as the last remnants were lifted, lots of sheltering field mice made their great escape and the boys and dogs ran in all directions after them.

Chapter Eleven – Football

Football was by far the main sport on the island, at school and inter-village. Dad was Manager of our area team, Kilchoman, for a few years, and Miss Campbell, our primary school teacher was treasurer. Home games were great, and we got to spend a Saturday evening in Port Charlotte at our local pitch. Rather than stand out in the cold, a lot of adults just sat in their cars along the touchline and sounded their horns when their team scored. There were two or three decent referees on the island but the two linesmen were usually an adult supporter from each team who was unlucky enough to arrive first. At really organised games such as cup matches, the linesman would get a flag but as often as not, his white handkerchief was used. Being a linesman was an absolutely thankless job: nobody agreed with their decisions, and with supporters standing virtually on the touchline, banter and arguments were rife.

We were sort of unofficial ballboys. We hung about behind the goals, having some good banter with the goalkeepers and having to run for the ball every time a shot at goal went wayward. It wouldn't be the first time that a goal was scored because the keeper, who'd had a quiet game, was distracted by us instead of watching the play going on in front of him.

There was every type of player taking part. Some were quite serious players who we idolised, there were some great athletes who could run faster than a hare but who couldn't kick a ball to save their lives, there were players who were picked as goalies and didn't even want to be there. Peter Pearce was the Jimmy Johnstone of his day, the most unlikely looking fast winger, but he didn't half weave through some defences. However, the atmosphere and the craic were terrific, and if the men went for a pint in the Lochindaal Hotel in Port Charlotte, then it meant we'd get to stay out later. What we didn't want to hear was Dad and some of the players, or people he met up with saying that they'd meet in the Abbotsford Hotel in Bruichladdich, because that meant he could dump me at the house first.

There was a café opposite Port Charlotte Hotel and that was an essential stopping off place on the way home from a match. Every single one of us had the same thing every single time: pie, beans and chips. I don't even know if they served anything else, we had our meal planned and that's all we were going to have. Away games, at Port Ellen for example, seemed like the other side of the world, but it was great to catch up with school friends from the other side of the island (or comically referred to as the wrong side of the island). After the match, we could go and get an ice cream, then we'd have to sit in the car while the men went for a pint. They thought that by bringing us out a tiny mixer bottle of Schweppes orange we'd be content sitting there like stooges.

A football tale I'd rather forget but will haunt me forever came about when I was ten and a half.

Remembering earlier when I spoke about poor television signals, the World Cup was on TV, and luckily the Distillery had guests staying in the Flat which had a state-of-the-art television set. The year was 1966 which will make even the most fanatical Scottish football fan weep. Dad and I were invited round to the Flat to watch a match almost every night for over three weeks. Our hosts looked after us impeccably, good conversation, plenty of drinks, and they put enough crisps in bowls on the coffee table to feed four people. Now, to a ten-year-old, if nibbles are placed in front of you, and someone says, 'Help yourself', and nobody's name is on the dishes, then surely it's every man (or boy) for himself. But no, apparently it's good manners and etiquette to pick at a crisp or two at your leisure throughout the evening. I ate the lot. I was told years later that it was quite embarrassing to witness.

But worse than that, at the risk of alienating English readers, England only went on and won the damn Cup. It didn't seem an issue at the time, but I still to this day cringe when I see pictures of a smug-looking Bobby Moore in his red strip, or Bobby Charlton with the world's worst comb-over, or Nobby Stiles with his toothless grin, dancing round Wembley with the trophy.

Kilchoman F.C. played in claret and blue vertical striped football shirts. So when I finished in Bowmore School and went to Dunoon Grammar School, Dad gave me one of the Kilchoman shirts for PE. Now I didn't realise that all the mainland boys at the school weren't as naive as me, in fact they were a lot more worldly wise. So, on the first day at PE, we sat in a row of benches in the gym and Mr Ferguson, our teacher, complimented the class on the fine array of football jerseys. He decided to start at one end of the row, and asked us to name the team whose shirt we were wearing.

First boy, 'Manchester United, Sir.'

Second boy, 'Rangers, Sir.'

Third boy, 'Chelsea, Sir.'

Fourth boy, 'Hearts, Sir.'

Fifth boy, aka little island teuchter, 'Kilchoman, Sir.'

Well, the place erupted into laughter. 'Where the hell is that?' they all seemed to shout in unison, mimicking my accent. I didn't even have the sense to pretend it was maybe a variation of an Aston Villa or West Ham strip as they wore similar colours. Needless to say, I went out and bought a Manchester United away strip (at that time, yellow jersey with blue collar and cuffs, and blue shorts) the next day.

Chapter Twelve – Bruichladdich Hall

Sandwiched between Greta's Post Office and the Fletcher's bungalow on the North side of the village was our Hall. Tuesday night was our badminton night and well attended by youngsters. The Hall was a perfect size for the badminton court, although high shots were a gamble as the rafters were so low. We played doubles mostly so that more people could be involved, and there was also a dart board set up in the passageway at the entrance door. One thing that dawns on me now is the trust that was part and parcel of our lives. There are so many stories about houses not being locked at night because the crime rate was zero, and the same trust was respected as far as the Hall was concerned. The keys used to hang on a hook in the front porch of Dr Tait's house and it was a case of the first person, children included, who arrived at the Hall simply went and helped themselves to the bunch of keys. No need to knock at the door, no-one checking who picked up the key, and they were always returned and never lost.

Thinking back, if you remember the habit we developed at primary school of saying, 'I don't know' at the start of every question, well, I developed a strange routine at home, but only, for some reason, on badminton nights. Our sofa at home was positioned across the living room. Dad would sit on it at night beside the fire with his dram and Daily Record newspaper. I always went to badminton, never ever got refused, but still went through a process of asking for permission. I always went to the kitchen, where Mum seemed to live, and interrupted her washing the dishes to ask if I could go to badminton.

‘Go and ask your father,’ was always the reply. So I duly went to the living room, walked all the way along quite a long room, round the back of the sofa, and asked the back of Dad’s head if I could go to badminton.

’Have you done your homework?’ he always said. I confirmed that I had.

’Okay then.’

Not the longest conversation in the world but I never worked out the reason for trudging all the way round the back of the sofa and never facing him to ask. I imagine he took great delight in watching this routine unfold at the same time every Tuesday and probably grinned behind his newspaper thinking ‘here we go again’ as I walked around him.

I’ve already mentioned the School Christmas Play and the Village Christmas Party, and the next biggest event that we got involved in was the WRI Sale of Work at harvest time. The perimeter of the Hall was set out with tables, and again the kids were trusted to open the Hall in the morning and also to be there to accept donations. The adults followed in due course. Although all sorts of produce, home baking and items were brought in, there was something magical about when local crofters turned up with boxes and sacks of vegetables. It makes you realise now how little character there is nowadays in supermarket produce departments. The beautiful-looking vegetables we received also smelled amazing. That aroma is definitely a childhood memory that is certainly missing in today’s mass-produced market.

I’m also amazed at myself and all similar-aged children from the village because as the women from the village and quite a big surrounding area came with home baking, we duly placed them on the tables in the main Hall. I don’t recall if we were tempted, but we never pinched a single biscuit.

Please don't put me in charge of such an event today at the age of sixty-seven, because I would definitely tuck in. Again, as per the produce, the cakes etc. looked gorgeous. Mrs McGillivray from Sunderland Farm baked legendary sponges.

I was always sure to have my pocket money with me before the Sale of Work started, and I'm afraid I homed in on tablet and fudge until I sickened myself, but of course still managed tea at night when we went home.

The Abbotsford Hotel always donated drinks and mixers and I remember we used to buy tiny yellow tins of Schweppes Indian Tonic. We must have thought we looked really cool drinking such 'adult' drinks.

In latter years of my childhood, probably from the late 60s, when Invergordon Distillers took over the Distillery, onwards, the Distillery used the Hall for their annual Dinner Dance. The highlight for us was the spectacle of the 'parade'. All the guests, looking immaculate, with men in suits or kilts and the ladies in long dresses, assembled in the Distillery Filling Store for pre-dinner drinks, then all walked together along the road to the Hall. They all walked in one big group, about six abreast across the whole road and traffic was stopped for the two hundred yard walk. It was spectacular and we'd all be outside seeing how many people we could recognise. Mum couldn't help herself, and made sure she was on the left-hand side of the parade, closest to our garden. 'Make sure he goes to bed at a decent time,' she'd say as she passed, to whoever was looking after me.

Chapter Thirteen – Return

In 2006, thirty-five years after leaving Islay to finish my education in Dunoon, I returned, courtesy of my employers, Diageo, who moved me after a four-year stint at Talisker Distillery on the Isle of Skye. There was a saying on Islay 'Never trust a Skye man' and I expected a similar tongue-in-cheek saying on Skye but no matter how many people at Talisker I told that to, no-one had heard of it. In fact, I was made very welcome as I was the first manager there for years who appreciated the unique nature of living and working on an island. Funnily enough, even with the luxury and good fortune at having a bridge, Skye retains an 'island' mentality. It was a bit ridiculous hearing some of our colleagues from Head Office, about a two and a half hours drive away in Elgin, complaining about having to come to Skye, as though there was some chance they were going to get stranded on such a remote location.

My first position was manager of Lagavulin Distillery, and I had a company house at Traigh Beag West, across the road from the Maltings in Port Ellen. Our company had thousands of employees worldwide but I don't think any had a more relaxing, scenic drive to work in the mornings. Mind you, the journey time used to be doubled because I always met Willie Currie in the lorry taking Lagavulin draff across the island. I wasn't allowed to just pass and wave. I was flagged down and we had to have a conversation about what he thought of the stillman he'd just been talking to, then how the industry and the world was changing (his favourite phrase about modern distilling was, 'Well boy, not in your father's day'), then I had to endure his joke of the day, and only then was I able to carry on driving. I could have left home at a different time, but I wouldn't have missed our morning chat for the world.

One thing I love is banter and returning through my work gave me a perfect opportunity to wind up my colleagues.

Diageo was formed in 1997 following the merger of two companies, Guinness and Grand Metropolitan. The newly invented word 'Diageo' comes from a Latin word 'dies' meaning 'Day', and the Greek word 'geo' meaning 'World'. No doubt someone was paid a fortune to come up with that one, but apparently it complements the company's slogan 'Celebrating Life, Every Day, Everywhere'. So Guinness were the owners of United Distillers, which owned Lagavulin, Caol Ila and Port Ellen Maltings, while Grand Metropolitan owned the company I worked for, J&B Scotland Limited.

Throughout Scotland, at the now thriving Diageo, there were around thirty distilleries and most had a healthy mix of employees from both the original companies.

However, in 2006, I was the only ex-J&B employee, coming to Islay to work with over forty ex-United Distillers workers. Better still, my Dad was a United Distillers employee in the 1950s and moved to J&B Scotland in the 70s so I always told people it was to better himself.

We were fiercely proud of our own original companies and brands so plenty of opportunities developed to wind people up. Although my original company had the bigger financial stake in the merger, we were far smaller in the number of distilleries we operated. We had four, to UD's twenty-eight.

Therefore, everyone on Islay was convinced that UD took us over, thanks mostly to the wind-up merchants in the engineering department, rather than it being a merger. I hope I got the final say on the day I left

Islay. There was a new meeting room created in the Engineering Centre at the Maltings so I spent a whole Sunday afternoon converting it into 'The J&B Suite' by adorning it in J&B promotional items like water jugs, coasters, whisky glasses, a mirror, clock etc.

I now had to acclimatise myself to living on the 'wrong' side of the island. The house has the most gorgeous view from the huge living room window, looking across Port Ellen Bay. I never tired of sitting watching the ferries, barley boats, cruise ships and yachts enter and leave the bay. Following my description, in Chapter Three, of witnessing the demise of the puffers when bulk malt arrived by lorry on the new roll-on/rolloff ferries, the barley boats in Port Ellen are yet another advancement in this ever-changing world. The boats carry in excess of a thousand tonnes of barley from East Anglia, and it's blown, via a big pipe, into storage silos on the pier.

After a couple of years at Lagavulin (yes, big companies never let you settle anywhere), I spent almost three years managing the Maltings. I lost my inspiring drive to work in the mornings but replaced it with a two-minute walk. In week three of my Maltings career the silo collapsed, causing the road to be closed and neighbours being vacated from their houses. Quite a baptism of fire for me, but having managed on Skye and Speyside also, I can assure you that Islay is the only place where I could have had so many people rally round to help me. Funnily enough, the day the silo collapsed, I was in Glasgow, getting the morning plane back home to Islay. I felt a tap on my shoulder on the plane and it was Gilby who said, 'I hear that one of your silos fell down; what happened?' I thought, well surely someone would have told me, so I said it probably wasn't anything serious and maybe it was just a small spill.

'Who told you?' I asked.

'Willie Shaw has just been on the phone,' Gilby said. 'He said the road's been closed and traffic diverted round the Link Road.'

Well, if there was a bigger teller of far-fetched stories than Willie on the island, I've yet to meet him. Unless you see it for yourself, take it with a pinch of salt. This is the man who one day claimed there was a round-bale feeder ring washed up at Gartmain and it had rolled along the seabed from Northern Ireland. But sure enough, when we flew over the Maltings, there was a sea of barley where there was once tarmac. Sorry Willie.

I had a lot of fun with the Distillery Managers team in a new rowing challenge that started, just as a way of getting people together on a Saturday afternoon, once a month. Cloudy and Marjory from Lagavulin allowed their white skiff Isis, initially purchased for the Pillage Malt fundraising, to be used for the events and this also became our training boat for weekly training evenings in Port Ellen Bay. Isis is an Egyptian Goddess by the way, just in case anyone thinks it was named after an unsavoury terrorist group. I also used the term 'training' evening because this conjures up a picture of serious rowers trying to hone their skills. Alas, after every session, our face muscles were sorer from laughing than our arm muscles were from rowing. A typical evening team was usually myself, Peter Campbell from the Maltings, John Campbell from Laphroaig, and Bruichladdich's own legend Duncan McGillivray. Duncan was the joker in the pack, ably backed up by Peter, and I remember one evening we thought we'd outsmart the rest of the teams by practising quickly manoeuvring around the buoy at the entrance to the bay. We reckoned we couldn't row as fast as some of the younger teams, but we'd use our experience to 'spin on a sixpence'. Each time we got a bit of speed up, and approached the buoy, two oars on one side would plunge into the water and the two rowers on the other side would row furiously. I mean the two rowers 'should' have rowed furiously. That was always Duncan's cue to crack a joke and we would hardly see through the tears, let alone skilfully spin the boat round. Everyone watching from the pontoons beside the pier must have been wondering why the great burst of speed was followed by a minute of non-rowing each time we tried to negotiate the buoy. I think apologies are due to all CalMac Ferry, barley boats and private yacht skippers who felt it safer to give way to us as we floundered around the bay.

I spoke about England's World Cup win haunting me and I inadvertently reminded myself about it during a Lagavulin Brand promotional tour in Tokyo in 2007. I took part in a whisky magazine interview and had previously been prompted to bring with me something nostalgic that I would 'always' take on tour. The interview, through an interpreter, went well and sure enough my host asked me if there was anything I couldn't travel without as he'd like to take a photograph of it.

I duly obliged and folded over the sleeve of my kilt jacket and proudly showed him my gold threepenny bit cufflinks. I told the guy that these had been presented to my Dad by Catto's Whisky Company. I padded out the story by telling him that I never went on stage without them and if I ever needed support during a presentation, I just looked at the cufflinks and felt my late Father's inspiration. Imagine my horror, when I looked intently at the cufflinks as they were being photographed, and in all the years since I inherited them, I hadn't noticed the year of issue on them – 1966. That year will haunt me for the rest of my life. I wonder if it's a coincidence that I've now inexplicably 'lost' them.

Two years at Lagavulin flew by. Again, big companies mistake a happy working environment and good morale for lack of progress and determination. What they see are production figures, targets, share prices, cash flow. What they don't see is goodwill, hard graft, good visitor experience, and the resourcefulness you need to make things work on an island. I don't care what anyone says, visitors love associating distilleries with people and changing managers frequently on sites with strong single malt brand connections is wrong.

I think my days in distilling were numbered in my own brain after a brand promotion trip to Japan. Fifteen to eighteen hours a day, in my kilt for seven straight days, promoting the brand as enthusiastically on the eighteenth hour as the first hour, only to come home and have my boss slap a white envelope on my desk and say, 'Well Graham, we're not offering you as big a pay rise as I would have liked.' Only a man who'd never been selected to represent the company on a hectic brand promotional tour could then follow that with, 'But you have had jollies to Japan after all.' It was during the financial collapse in 2008: the pay 'rise', as he called it, was zero.

Talking of Japan, I'm not the world's greatest computer and technology buff, but our Mum just didn't get technology at all. On one occasion when I went to Tokyo, I was doing my promotional duties as soon as I landed and I met a Japanese journalist who was a regular visitor to Islay. Of course, we had the customary photographs taken, and he immediately emailed them to Christine Logan. Being a great friend of our family, Christine printed the picture and took it round to Mum's house in Bowmore. Taking into account the time difference, this all happened on the same day.

Mum opened the door and Christine said, 'Hello May, I've just brought you a picture of Graham.'

Mum said, 'Oh I'm sorry Christine, Graham's not in, he'll be away for a while.' After being told it was a picture of Graham today, Mum said it couldn't possibly be today because I was in Japan. Poor Mum was still living in the age of sending your camera spool to Kodak or Truprint and waiting a week for your pictures. Needless to say, that photo found its way into the hands of the Engineers at the Maltings so by the time I got home a week later, it was on my office wall and altered to have me wearing a white Japanese flag as a headdress.

If you Google 'Mark Gillespie Islay Feis', and open The Feis Ile Series, and scroll down to Episode 263, you'll come across a one-hour podcast interview I did during Feis Ile 2010. In it, Mark asked me if I was sorry that we'd lost some famous distilleries over the years, like Port Ellen for example, and wasn't it a great shame that stocks of their single malts were dwindling. I explained to him that some distilleries like Brora, Rosebank, and Port Ellen weren't popular with malt whisky enthusiasts until they were closed for various business reasons and I made the knowledgeable revelation that Port Ellen Distillery would never reopen. Here we are in 2023 and the new Port Ellen Distillery is nearing completion. What do I know!!

Modern distilleries have changed beyond recognition since my childhood and yes, I get it, the world is evolving but it is pretty sad that characters and personalities are not encouraged any more. Total staff at a big (and ever expanding) distillery now is more likely to be in single figures rather than twenty or thirty. Nothing in the world can afford not to change, but it's just that little bit sad to witness it on Islay where people and life are friendlier, more relaxed and more fulfilled than on the mainland. Everyone is entitled to their opinion on where distilling is headed and how many distilleries or whisky-making facilities Islay can sustain. Whisky distilleries that can make different 'characters' of spirit, people who can reach managerial positions and have never rolled a cask, it's all too much, too quick.

I loved when some of my mainland-based colleagues visited Islay for work reasons. They hated the fact that they felt trapped on the island and almost went into panic mode if their ferry or plane threatened not to depart on a Friday afternoon. They hated the travelling, the roads, the lack of shops, the logistics of getting spares to Islay. I revelled in saying to them that it's the things they can't stand about an island, that are the things we love about Islay. I openly admit I regretfully left the industry because, after several years as a manager, and having it drummed into me that my priority was to encourage the 'change' culture in all employees, I discovered it was actually me who couldn't change.

I once wrote an article for a whisky magazine, but it never reached publication, about simple, annoying things like words and names that had crept into our very traditional industry. I was a distillery manager for seventeen years, and actually, not once was my official title ever Distillery Manager. At Glenspey I was Production Supervisor, at Benrinnes and Talisker it was Site Operations Manager, at Lagavulin I became Distilling Manager, and with William Grant at Balvenie, followed by Glenfiddich my title was Team Leader. As if that isn't enough to make me roll my eyes, imagine the hairs on the back of my neck standing to attention when Washbacks have suddenly become Fermenters, aaaaargh.

Another break from my idea of tradition distilling ways occurred just before I retired. A very good friend of mine was a Brand Ambassador and before he retired, he made sure that I was told, and applied for his job. It sounded like fate to me. Surely someone with distilling experience, who lived in distilleries from childhood, and with stories of Islay from schooling to Distillery Management would have been ideal to spread the word globally. Alas, at my post-interview meeting, after being told that someone with a sales background had got the job, I was informed that it was easier (in the company's eyes) to teach a marketeer about distilling than the other way round. Ah well, that's life.

After leaving Islay again in 2011, I got my mojo back and managed Balvenie & Kininvie Distilleries for a year, then Glenfiddich Distillery for two years, and felt a refreshing family run atmosphere about the place, but sadly in three short years it became a mini version of the bigger multinational companies and the modern trend of 'production comes first, and people, personalities and morale come second' wasn't for me.

Chapter Fourteen – Conclusion

I think I had quite a privileged childhood in Bruichladdich. I certainly benefited forty years later when giving presentations or whisky tastings as a manager myself on Islay because my stories of being brought up at a distillery gave me a lot of credibility. Grant Carmichael and I used to do quite a little double act at Lagavulin in 2007/2008 where he would tell visitors his tales of being a manager and he'd describe going to Bruichladdich Distillery to see Dad and meeting Peter's nine-year-old son who couldn't keep out of mischief. I used to kneel beside Grant and he'd pretend to 'clip' my ear and he'd say, 'Yes that's exactly the height you were then.'

I hope I've shown just how much the village, and in reality the whole island, changed with the introduction of the roll-on/roll-off ferries and life was made easier. Unfortunately the number of jobs was vastly reduced, and the whole ambience of the island changed. The demise of the puffers, mail boats and cargo boats in particular was very rapid, virtually overnight, and the jobs lost must have affected both those ashore and the seamen. Anyone who sailed on the *Lochiel* will have an affectionate or scary story or memory, but can you even recall the name, let alone any memorable event, on every roll-on/roll-off ferry since? I can't. One regret is that I never thought to ever enquire where any of our boats ended up. There would have been opportunities around the country to at least see some of them working a different route. The easiest one for me would have been to visit the *Lochiel* when I was in the RAF in South Wales, about an hour from Bristol, and it would have been quite nostalgic to have seen her as a restaurant. Unfortunately, everyone now enjoys, and is used to, faster ferries with five crossings a day in the summer, two planes a day, and faster turnarounds. But with easier access comes a faster pace of life and just a different lifestyle.

I lived on Skye for four years at the time of the charges being removed from the new Skye Road Bridge. They had an even more dramatic effect of the easier, free access to their island. Published figures showed a dramatic increase in crime for example, close to the areas adjacent to the bridge.

With my Dad being the Distillery Manager, I did have access to more parts of the plant than a lot of others and it may not seem a big deal to youngsters nowadays, but privileged chances to be driven about in draff and malt lorries was exciting in an age before mobile phones and electronic games. I remember standing on the barley boat *Shetland Trader* in Port Ellen one summer's evening with Peter Hart and as we looked along the shoreline and buildings in Port Ellen, he told me tales of all the mischief he and his friends got up to. (We felt a bit like Jack and Victor from 'Still Game' on TV). As he seemed to point out every building, in turn, along the village front, it appeared nobody had escaped some sort of pranks over the years. I jokingly asked him if he could imagine in fifty years' time, two old blokes like us would stand where we were standing and tell each other of memories of texting and video-calling each other from opposite ends of the village.

It's unfortunate that children nowadays can't experience the simple lifestyle we had in the 1960s, but that probably is the same story across the country, just more noticeable on an island. The exact same scenario is around today with anyone who joins a distillery workforce and wasn't able to experience the community, the characters, and the fun that used to make up a distillery.

AUTHOR BIO:

Born in Aberdeen, Graham Logie moved to Islay with his family when he was 5 years old. Graham completed six and a half years at Gortan Primary School followed by 4 years at Bowmore School before leaving the island. Graham tells of his upbringing in Bruichladdich and his love for the village and Islay are evident. Being the Distillery Manager's son gave him access to the distillery, and provided him with an insight into distilling which stood him well in his own career as a Distillery and Maltings Manager. Graham returned to Islay for a five year spell in 2006 before moving to manage Glenfiddich Distillery prior to his retirement. Today he lives near Bath in Somerset but visits his sisters on Islay at every opportunity.